G.A. Custer

to the Little Big Horn

STEVE ALEXANDER

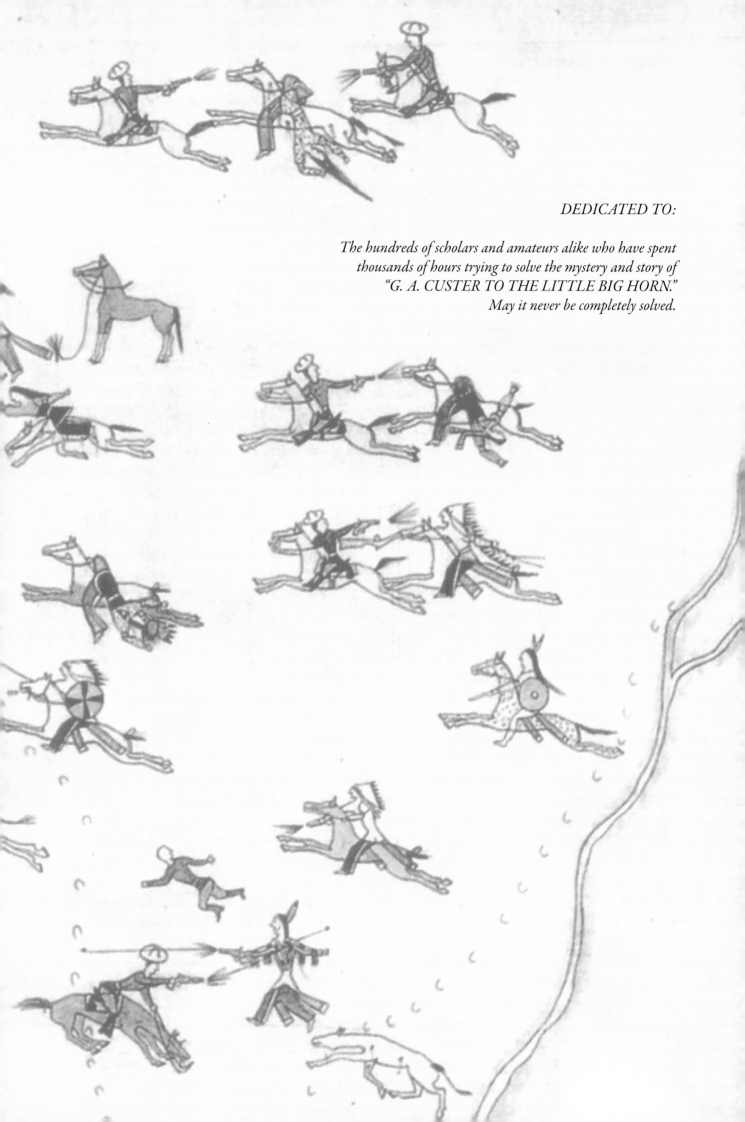

DEDICATED TO:

*The hundreds of scholars and amateurs alike who have spent
thousands of hours trying to solve the mystery and story of
"G. A. CUSTER TO THE LITTLE BIG HORN."
May it never be completely solved.*

Author
STEVE ALEXANDER

Design and typesetting
ANDREA PRESS

Published by
ANDREA PRESS
C/ Talleres, 21
Pol. Ind. de Alpedrete 28430 Alpedrete (Madrid)
Tel.: 91 857 00 08
Fax: 91 857 00 48
www.andrea-miniatures.com andrea@andrea-miniatures.com

Printed in SPAIN
Gráficas Díaz Turidi (Bilbao)

With thanks to:
Sandy Alexander
American Heritage Archives
James Aplan
Arizona Historical Society, Tucson
The Athenaeum - Interactive Online: www.the-athenaeum.org
Sandy Barnard
The *Bismarck Tribune*
Libby Coyner, Sharlot Hall Museum
Rowland Chenez
Mark Churms
Custer Battlefield Museum Garryowen, Montana. www.custermuseum.org
Dakota Territorial Museum Photographic Archives
Mary Desson
Gallon Historical Art
Father Vince Heier
Ralph Heinz
Ken Hendricksen, www.civilwarartist.com
William Heyen
Kansas Historical Society
Paul Houser
John Hurless
Judy Justus
Chris Kortlander
Chris Kull, Monroe County Historical Museum
John Langellier
Ernie and Sonja LaPointe
Robert R. Lende
Liberty Heritage Society Museum
Little Big Horn National Museum
M. John Lubetkin
Ernest Lyle Reedstrom
Joe Medicine Crow
Monroe County Historical Museum Archives
National Portrait Gallery, Smithsonian Institution
Ron Nichols
Lee Noyes
Ohio Historical Society
Martin Pate, www.pateart.com
Payette Collection, *Monroe Evening News*
Glen Peterman
Louis Pfeiffer
Ron C. Pickard
The Real Bird Family
Rick Reeves
Norm Sauer
Steve Shaw
Ken Smith
Smithsonian Institution, Washington DC
Pat Stevens and the Norvell Churchill Family
Michael Schreck
Tracy Stivers, www.donstivers.com
Glenwood Swanson
E. Leroy Van Horne
West Point Special Collections & Archives, USMC Library
Woolaroc Museum, Bartlesville, Oklahoma.

ISBN: 978-84-96658-28-8
D.L.: BI-3106-2010

Index

EDITOR'S NOTE:

The literary style and -in some cases- even the spelling used by the author in writing this book is a faithful recreation of the way G.A. Custer expressed himself in writing and talking. By retrieving terms, sayings and grammatical constructions in vogue during late 19th century, Steve Alexander brings the reader to the true essence of the Old West.

G. A. Custer.
By C. Gómez.

Preamble

I am very pleased to introduce Dr. Joseph Medicine Crow, Last War Chief of the Crow Tribe and recent recipient of the Presidential Medal of Freedom, two Bronze Stars and the French Legion of Honor Medal. Joe, whose Indian name is High Bird, is a native of Montana and the grandson of Custer's Crow Scout, White Man Runs Him. A military veteran, Joe served with the 103rd Infantry Division during World War II and was the last Crow to become a War Chief, having earned all four warrior honors in combat against the German Army. He was awarded the Bronze Star and the Legion d'honneur for his service in the military. Joe holds a Master's Degree in Anthropology and is the author of numerous books and articles including Counting Coup, Medicine Crow: The Handbook of the Crow Indians Law and Treaties, and From the Heart of Crow Country. He has appeared in numerous documentaries and films and is the Crow Tribal Historian, traveling and lecturing across the United States on the history of his tribe and the conflict of the Little Big Horn. In 1969 he wrote the script for Custer's Last Stand, the annual reenactment held in Hardin, Montana, each year during the anniversary of the Battle. He and the author have appeared in several documentaries together. On the anniversary of the Battle in June 2000, Joe bestowed upon the author the Crow name, Son of the Morning Star.

Christopher Kortlander
Founding Director - Custer Battlefield Museum
Garryowen, Montana
www.custermuseum.org

Joe Medicine Crow. 2008. Courtesy of Ron Nichols

Joe Medicine Crow bestows the name, "Son of the Morning Star" on the author June 25, 2000.
Photo courtesy of Robert R. Lende.

Introduction
by Joe Medicine Crow

"Why another Custer Book? "

I asked that question over a one hundred times during my lifetime.

Since I was a young man I have seen a thousand books published on General Custer. I've even written a few myself. When I was at USC, in one of the studios, I was even asked to help write the screenplay for "They Died With Their Boots On." I ended up being fired from the film company because I was writing the truth. Seems like the 100 or so Custer movies haven't always been concerned with the truth.

I've known Mr. Steve Alexander for over two decades and all the time I've known him he has tried to portray the truth of Custer and the Nomadic people Americans popularly call "Indians."

As an Indian, I grew up hearing the stories told by my Great-grandfather, White Man Runs Him who was one of Custer's Scouts. They say Custer regarded White Man Runs Him, the youngest of the six scouts, as the most reliable and likeable young man. So he [Custer] was proud of him. White Man Runs Him was ready to die with him [Custer]. Those who scouted for Custer wrote about him. They say he was rough on his soldiers, his men, but with the Crow Indians he was good to them. So they gave him the name, Son of the Morning Star. He was handsome, highly visible, so they gave him that honor, Son of the Morning Star. You know, Son of the Morning Star is bright, visible. So that is a pretty name. I've talked and listened to the stories of the Lakota and Cheyenne who fought in the 1876 battle. I wrote the script of "Custer's Last Stand" where for many years Steve Alexander rode as General Custer. For over a decade he has ridden in the reenactment that is put on each year at Medicine Tail Coulee - the exact spot where the Battle took place.

When I have watched Mr. Alexander in the reenactments and the many films he has appeared in, I have felt I was watching Son of the Morning Star. More than Errol Flynn or any other Hollywood actor, Mr. Alexander has captured the essence of who Son of the Morning Star was. It is because of that I bestowed the name of IKA' DIEUX' DAKA, Son of the Morning Star on him in 2000.

So it was my honor as a tribal historian, and an elder that I was in the position to give him [Mr. Alexander] that name. I give names. Not every Indian can give names. That is a sacred thing. So I think that was a good thing. That I gave Mr. Alexander that name.

We get along pretty good. Just like White Man Runs Him and Custer got along pretty good. They were good friends and Mr. Alexander and myself are pretty good friends. Mr. Alexander even looks like Custer, himself.

Only one other person has been given that name before Mr. Alexander.

Because he has dedicated his life to the history of Custer and the Indians, I think it fitting that I was asked to write this Introduction. I feel I know the Spirit of this Man. For an old Man to ask, "Why another Custer book? " because of the 1000 or more Custer books they never quite got the character of the man the Crow so aptly named Son of the Morning Star.

I am glad I have lived to see the day Mr. Alexander captures in these pages who Custer was, because Mr. Alexander is the Spirit of Son of the Morning Star.

May He Ride True & May He Ride Forever.

White Man Runs Him.
Joe's Grandfather.

Sometimes it's easier to write a book than to title it. Not so this time. "G. A. Custer" the General's own signature begins the title of this book. Very rarely did Custer sign anything "Custer" or "G. Custer" but rather "G.A. Custer." This personalized or validated all his orders or official correspondence.

While, TO THE LITTLE BIG HORN in rich red western style letters is symbolic of Custer's famous Red Tie; it is as well applicable to the Red Man, the characterization of the Nomadic People.

Brought together "G. A. Custer To The Little Big Horn" is almost an accounting, a letter, a paper or an explanation of this terse.

When the "Far West" steamboat returned to Fort Lincoln, on board was G. A. Custer's final installment of "War Memoirs he'd hoped to complete for Galaxy Magazine. Had he survived the Little Big Horn, he would have authored an article if not a complete book about this subject as well; reflecting on the success or failure of this event. I believe even if he had not perished, Little Big Horn like the Washita would then determine his future strategies in the warfare against the Plains Indians.

Therefore, "G. A. Custer To The Little Big Horn" is a study, but it is also a time line. "G. A. Custer" announces his birth, "To The Little Big Horn" is his journey.

How does G. A. Custer stack up or relate to the Little Big Horn? Both have received more than fifteen minutes of fame. Both reverberate through the conscience of history Internationally.

Custer is yet known worldwide without the attached "Little Big Horn."

But mention Little Big Horn and dare someone not to think of Custer.

Custer is to the Little Big Horn as Black is to White. Black can stand alone, but against the back drop of a white surface, black takes on a life, a prominence that becomes the focal point surrounded by the white surface. Conger then this image of Custer surrounded by Indians.

Little Big Horn is used because it is the proper spelling of that area. The Lakota referred to that valley as Pa Zees La Wak Pa, the Greasy Grass. The early Trappers and Mountain Men called it the Big Horn. The smaller river was the Little Horn. Where the two came together was the area known as the Little Big Horn.

Almost as an afterthought to diminish its significance, modern political correctness has dubbed it "Little Bighorn." Two words that do not do justice to the significance that affected the lives of the soldiers who fought, those who died and the Indians' way of life that was forever changed by the battle that took place on that hallowed piece of ground.

Little Big Horn spoken in the cadence of three drum beats marks the last three days of Custer's life commencing when the columns split and he rode out of the

Foreword

bottoms toward his appointment with destiny on the lonely slopes above the Little Big Horn River.

Little Bighorn reflects a past that white America shuns and would like to forget. For a nomadic people Little Big Horn was a victory, but it also ushered an ultimate defeat. Though insignificant as a battle, it validates and clarifies today's Native Americans.

Just as we reflect on Ancient History as B. C. or A. D., so too does it become a point in time to identify and recount the oral history of the tribes.

Without Custer the American Indian would have an entirely different definition of who they are today. Understanding "G. A. Custer To The Little Big Horn" is understanding who we are as a people today. Not only Indians, but Non Indians.

A better explanation of this phenomenon is richly covered in Michael Elliott's wonderful work "Custerology." Even Vine Deloria's "Custer Died for Your Sins" touched on this idea, if only in title alone. Therein lies the tome, "G. A. Custer To The Little Big Horn."

More than a History of the General himself, but a haunting reflection of ourselves.

And finally, in my dedication, I conclude with the statement, "May it never be completely solved."

In the one hundred and thirty some years that I have Followed the Guidon, I have traversed the country in quest of this Holy Grail of Custeriana.

If early on I had discovered the absolute truth my quest would have ended and I would have turned my attention to some other mystery, the Bermuda Triangle or Disappearance of Amelia Earhart; and not have made the friendships and smaller discoveries that are on the periphery of this exciting time in Our Country's History.

The Custer story is interconnected with so many facets that were the Industrial Age and evolution of the Frontier.

When the Civil War began it seemed his fame was instantaneous. George Armstrong Custer fought in every major engagement of the Army of the Potomac, but for the Battles of Fredericksburg and Chancellorsville.

For a majority of the battles he was in the front on horseback leading sixty successful charges and being unhorsed eleven times but with few scratches. Some thought he led a charmed life. A life filled with action and excitement that was to end at only thirty six years of age, yet achieving more than most men who might have lived twice as long.

Why do we remember Custer? Why does his name ignite controversy and discussion even after a century and a half when he walked the earth?

He represents the success story spawned and woven through novels and film. Humble beginnings to Rock Star notoriety. He wrote: "In years long numbered with the past, when I was verging upon manhood, my every thought was ambitious-not to be wealthy, not to be learned, but to be great. I desired to link my name with

acts and men, and in such a manner as to be a mark of honor- not only to the present, but to future generations."[1]

His fame might have been extinguished had he not graduated from West Point at the outbreak of the War and been assigned to the front. Had not Sheridan adopted the impetuous Boy General and assigned him to the newly formed 7th Cavalry, he may have been only remembered as the half or so dozen generals who'd fought in America's bloodiest war.

After that war Custer and the West became the perfect marriage. Realization of the novels he'd cut his teeth on as a small boy, the Boy General metamorphosed into the Plainsman described by James Fenimore Cooper. And as if overnight he grew and adapted to the hunt and assimilated into the society of scouts, Plainsmen and nomadic tribes that inhabited the west.

"Custer cut a cutting from a dead Indian and grafted it onto himself. 'Look,' he said, standing there with his arms wide and though that extra slip of carrion attached to his chest were an orchard.

But the graft did take. We could see it swell, day by day during the campaign until he had to keep his shirt unbuttoned. The tree, or whatever it was, branched out up under his chin, and he was proud of every bud, but wondered aloud how long this could continue.

Then, one morning, he woke with shadows in those limbs, hundreds of cocoons, so went to work with shears, reverting to his old self again."[2]

In the aged and lined faces of a people photographed by Edward S. Curtis, Custer felt comfort and identity; strong breezes that gusted across the prairie uplifted his soul and brought meaning to his destiny.

As dawn approached the Centennial of our Nation a melancholy enveloped the Frontier.

Change and technology-the end of mystery and myth-shrinking the expanse-rails being laid in the scratched earth worn by travois.

The Little Big Horn was the end of an era for a Native People on the Plains and the beginning of a blend of fact and fantasy spawned by the people who lived it in truth or imagination.

Buffalo Bill's Wild West set the tone for those who followed in film and novel. Striving to tell a tale that almost achieved the brass ring of reality-but when in doubt printed the romance of what our hearts wished it had been.

To analyze the prism from all angles is more ambitious than these pages contained herein. The bibliography is but a start.

My goal is to reflect and hopefully open the door to those who wish to begin a journey whether on a Conestoga wagon or the "Jupiter Locomotive" coursing across the grasslands, cutting a swath in the herds that were the life blood of a civilization that once was and now are all but vanished.

Steve Alexander

'Visions of Glory'. By Richard S. Headley, 1992. Courtesy of Custer Battlefield Museum, Garryowen. Montana.

G. A. Custer: The Man

" ...George A. Custer, dressed in a dashing suit of buckskin, is prominent everywhere... flitting to and fro, in his quick eager way, taking in everything connected with his command,... with the keen, incisive manner for which he is so well known. The General is full of perfect readiness for a fray with the hostile red devils." So was the description by Mark Kellogg in his first column for the Bismarck Tribune on May 17, 1876.[3]

Elizabeth Custer remembered her husband as "...a figure that would have fixed attention anywhere. He had a marked individuality of appearance, ... not the least out of place on the frontier. He wore troop boots reaching to his knees, buckskin breeches fringed on the sides, a dark navy blue shirt with a broad collar, and a red necktie whose ends floated over his shoulder exactly as they did when he and his entire division of cavalry had worn them during the war. He was at this time thirty-five years of age, weighed one hundred and seventy pounds, and was nearly six feet in height. His eyes were clear blue and deeply set; his hair, short, wavy, and golden in tint. His mustache was long and tawny in color; his complexion was florid, except where his forehead was shaded by his... broad felt hat, that was almost a sombrero... for the sun always burned his skin ruthlessly.

He was the most agile, active man I ever knew, ...Horse and man seemed one when the general vaulted into the saddle. ...Yet every nerve was alert and like finely tempered steel, for the muscles and sinews that seemed so pliable were equal to the curbing of the most fiery animal."[4]

These descriptions might sooner have been ascribed to Errol Flynn the dashing actor of the cinema who brought to life on screen the adventures of G. A. Custer in "They Died With Their Boots On." For many he epitomized the "Boy General" in swashbuckling flamboyance. Students of Custeriana often claim this film was their introduction to the story and lifelong interest in the Battle of the Little Big Horn. If there had not been such a man in real life, Hollywood would have invented him.

"Custer's face was not the face of a thoughtless, impulsive man." Wrote Annie Gibson Roberts, "it was the somewhat worn, but eager countenance of a man who had faced extraordinary responsibilities in youth; his eyes penetrating, his broad, massive brow was the brow of a thinker-not one who would rush into danger simply for the glory of it.

Errol Flynn as G. A. Custer in his exceptional portrayal for Warner Bros
"They Died With Their Boots On" 1940.
Courtesy of John Langellier.

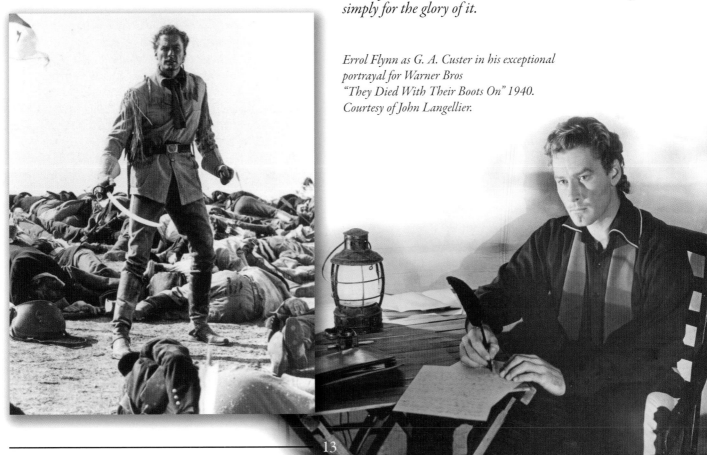

'Custer with his dogs'. By A. Berghaus.

Custer talked very fast in a nervous, energetic way, and this with the fact that his face was mobile and expressive, may have given to strangers the impression that he was impulsive, but he was a rapid reasoner and in a few moments grasped a situation and weighed and acted upon it... Custer possessed a happy nature; there was a great deal of the lighthearted good spirits of a boy in him..."

"One never to be forgotten afternoon" Annie watched as the general rocked his girl wife in a hammock, then turned to her and exclaimed, *"Annie, I'm the happiest man in the world! I envy no one. With my dear little wife whom I adore and the 7th Cavalry, the proudest command in the world, I would not change places with a King."* [5]

"General Custer riding at the head of the column, seeing the nest of a meadow-lark, with birdlings in it, in the grass, guided his horse around it, and resumed the straight course again without saying a word or giving a direction. The whole command of many hundred cavalrymen made the same detour, each detachment coming up to the place where the preceding horsemen had turned out, and looking down into the nest to find the reason for the unusual departure from the straight line of march." [6]

"...he was a frequent observer, even admirer, of the qualities of some animals which made them particularly notable specimens of their species." [7] "...all knew the general's love of pets." From a field mouse he kept in an ink well on his desk to "...a badger, porcupine, raccoon, prairie dog, and a wild turkey, all served their brief time as members of our family... When a ferocious wildcat was brought in... it was kept in the cellar. Mary used to make many retreats, tumbling up the stairs, when the cat flew at her the length of its chain." [4]

"Custer was rarely without his dogs. They accompanied him on hunts and on campaigns; they ranged themselves at his feet, rested their heads on his lap, shared his bed and his food, got under foot, made nuisances of themselves, but never lost their special place in his affection." [8]

"Before he had been long in the West, he saw that the redman was the victim of a vicious circle that was closing in on him and choking out his very life. The settlers, the railroads, the pioneers, the cattlemen demanded more and more land that belonged to the Indians. To get this land, the government brought the Indians into peace councils, where they bribed them with presents and promises until they would sign away their rights. Then, forced to their reservations, more often than not they were cheated out of their annuities, their rations and clothing, by an unscrupulous Indian agent." [9]

"When we first beheld the redman, we beheld him in his home of peace and plenty, the home of nature. Sorrows furrowed lines were not weakened by being forced to sleep in dreary caves and deep morasses, fireless, comfortless and coverless, through fear of the hunter's deadly rifle. His heart did not quake with terror at every gust of wind that sighed through the trees, but on the contrary, they were the favored sons of nature, and she like a doting mother, had bestowed all her gifts on them. They stood in the native strength and beauty, stamped with the proud majesty of free born men, whose souls never knew fear, or whose eyes never quelled beneath the fierce glance of men. But what are

General Custer's birthplace. New Rumley. Ohio.

they now, those monarchs of the west? They are like withered leaves of their own native forest, scattered in every direction by the fury of the tempest." [10]

"The only good Indian I ever saw was dead." corrupted to *"The only Good Indian is a Dead Indian"* [11]

"The Redman is alone in his misery. The earth is one vast desert to him. Once it had its charms to lull his spirit to repose, but now the home of his youth, the familiar forests, under whose grateful shade, he and his ancestors stretched their weary limbs after the excitement of the chase, are swept away by the axe of the woodman; the hunting grounds have vanished from his sight and in every object he beholds the hand of desolation. We behold him now on the verge of extinction, standing on his last foothold, clutching his blood-stained rifle, resolved to die amidst the horrors of slaughter, and soon he will be talked of as a noble race who once existed but now have passed away." [10]

"We are placed between two fires" General William T. Sherman wrote [12] The Indians not on reservations *"are hostile and will remain so until killed off."*

"Custer had a heart like an Indian; if we ever left out one thing in our ceremonies he always suggested it to us." [13]

"Custer, you are the only man that never failed me." General Philip H. Sheridan, Fort Leavenworth, 1869. [14]

Thus painted the portrait of Custer the man, and set in motion the dichotomy of legend; conflicted by his love of the West, his admiration of the American Indian, and his sense of duty to Country. All of this would reach an almost operatic crescendo of eagle bone whistles and screams in the final moments along the banks of the Little Big Horn River in Montana Territory. Hardly a person doesn't know how it ended; popularized primarily by the most viewed piece of art known to man, the Cassilly Adams/Otto Becker painting of "Custer's Last Fight." Distributed by Anheuser-Busch in a stellar marketing ploy second to none throughout the saloons and drinking establishments around the world, resulting in more people having seen that painting than any other work of art since more people go to bars than art galleries.

Many have capitalized on the phenomenon, but what really gave birth to the legend? Where did the physical man come from?

In a letter written to his wife from New York on April 23, 1876 George Custer wrote: *"I received a letter from a gentleman at Kirkwall, in the Orkneys, of the name Custer. He traces our relationship to the family, back to 1647, and gives the several changes the name has undergone, -Cursetter, Cursider, Cusiter, Custer, all belonging to the same parish... He writes... I am convinced we are of the same stock..."* [15]

Tradition held he was of Teutonic ancestry, yet the General may have ridden to his death believing his family had genealogical roots extending back to a group of seventy bleak islands off the north-eastern coast of Scotland. [16]

The Custer Family was convinced for a long time they were kin to the First President of the United States George Washington through the Ball Family; Sarah Martha Ball wife of Paul Custer being the sister (in reality Cousin) of Mary Ball Washington. [17]

Maria Kirkpatrick Custer.

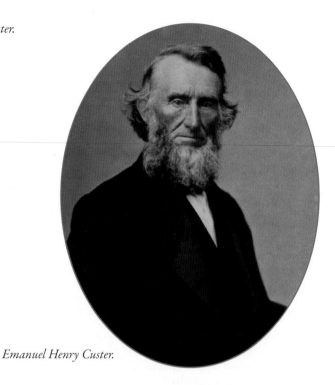

Emanuel Henry Custer.

However, Albert Faust purports, Custer's ancestor was a Hessian Soldier paroled in 1778 following Burgoyne's surrender and shortly thereafter settling in Pennsylvania. Faust's book "German Element in the United States" claims the soldier changed his name, making for easier pronunciation amongst his English speaking neighbors and perhaps removing the stigma attached to Hessian Mercenaries of the British Crown.[18]

The Castor Association of America noted for their extensive research and genealogical study of the Custer family claimed they first immigrated to America in the late 17th Century from the Rhineland of Germany. Their surname originally "Kuester" went through a variety of changes, Kiester, Gerster, Kustard before settling on the now more familiar spelling. George Armstrong Custer was a direct great-great-great-grandson of Paulus and Gertrude Kuester from Crefeld, Kaldenkirchen, Duchy of Juelich (today North Rhine-Westphalia state), who settled in Germantown, Pennsylvania possibly around 1700.[19]

Custer's mother Maria Ward, at the age of 16, married Israel Kirkpatrick. who died in 1835. A year later she married Emanuel Henry Custer, also a widower, both having children from their first marriages. Maria's grandparents, George Ward and Mary Ward (née Grier) were from County Durham, England. Their son James Grier Ward was born in Dauphin, Pennsylvania and married Catherine Rogers, and their daughter, Maria being The General's mother.

Catherine Rogers was the daughter of Thomas Rogers and Sarah Armstrong; thought at one time to be the provocation for the General's middle name. Although in all likelihood it was George Armstrong, a Methodist Minister, who stayed beside Maria during child birth with family hopes the child might someday become part of the clergy.

George Armstrong Custer drew his first breath of air, in the late evening of Thursday, December 5, 1839 and came into the world on the kitchen table, assisted by Jane Lyle in New Rumley, Harrison County, Ohio during a desperate snow storm. So crippling were the effects of the blizzard that the local doctor, only a few miles away in New Market, wasn't able to get up the hill in time. Maria frail and careworn from the loss of two previous infants was incapable of climbing the stairs to the second floor bedroom and weathered the hard delivery with prayers and encouragement from the local minister.[20]

Throughout his life Custer was known by a variety of flattering and not so flattering of nicknames. He was called alternately Armstrong or "Autie" (an early mispronunciation of his middle name.) Cadets at West Point christened him "Fanny" or "Cinnamon" from the ubiquitous scent of his hair oil. The Press called him "The Boy General" while the names "Ole Curley" and "Jack" (a phonetic of his initials GAC usually stenciled on his trunks and satchel) were chosen by soldiers in his Civil War Commands in preference to "Hard Ass" or "Glory Hunter" used disparagingly by his troops in the 7th Cavalry. When he went west, the Plains Indians referred to him as "Long Hair" or "Yellow Hair" indiscriminately. The Osage called him "Ouchess" the Creeping Panther while his Crow scouts bestowed upon him the name, "Son of the Morning Star."

Custer's father, Emanuel, the local Blacksmith and Justice of the peace; was known for his strong Lutheran faith and opinionated political views, balanced by an exuberant sense of humor that became a trademark of all Custers who were to follow.

Jacob Custer, Emanuel's brother who surveyed and platted the town of New Rumley in 1813 and another Uncle George, who later became a blacksmith in Monroe, Michigan were also influential in "Autie's" childhood.[21]

But it was Doctor Black[22] who pulled Autie's first baby tooth for which Emanuel remembered after braving up, the boy to exclaim, "Pop, you and me can whip all the Whigs in Ohio!"[23]

Quite liked and well respected around Harrison County, Emanuel was duly elected to the position of commander of the "New Rumley Invincibles" the unit charged with putting down the then nonexistent Indian problems. Thoroughly familiar with the Manual of Arms, Young Armstrong was ever present at drill with carved wooden musket and a small military uniform sewn by his mother and Half Sister Lydia Ann Kirkpatrick.[24]

Ann who was much older, became a second mother to Autie and was largely responsible for the families' move to Monroe, Michigan when Armstrong was about 2 1/2 years old. Site of the "River Raisin Massacre," Monroe the northern town of 3,000 inhabitants was five days travel by horse from New Rumley across rough and broken roads.[25]

Elizabeth Clift Bacon
1855

By that time Autie had been joined by a younger brother Nevin Johnson, who was barely a year old when discouraged by having had their livestock rustled, the family pulled up stakes and shut down the blacksmith shop returning to Harrison County.[26]

When younger brothers Thomas Ward and Boston arrived the Custer family was living on a farm in a hollow just west of New Rumley. Besides the big house and a large accommodating barn for their horses and cattle, they raised crops, chickens and sold eggs. Their family pet, a red dog named Rainger kept the fox out of the chicken coop.[22]

Margaret Emma, whom they called Maggie, was the last of the brood arriving on June 5, 1852.[17]

Separated in the fields so they would work rather than talk, the Custer boys were always into one kind of mischief after another. Even a onetime make shift rodeo came to an abrupt end when an unwilling steer turned bronco and threw Armstrong off.

Harsh winters and long summers forged the physical stamina that the Custer boys became famous for. Armstrong himself excelled in sports as evidenced when he walked to Cadiz to compete in a foot race at the fairgrounds. After winning first place, an award of two bits, he ran desperately home to present the prize to his mother. The excursion, a round trip of 20 miles over hills and ungroomed trails hardly affecting this strapping youth.[27]

'Coming Events Cast Their Shadows Before'.
Cassilly Adams 1886. Arizona Historical Society, Tucson.

District Five School House. Cadiz, Ohio.

The closeness and tender heartedness of the Custer family was exhibited openly in their humor, wit, and affection for one another. But it was the closeness Armstrong shared with his mother, long enduring and later recounted when Libbie wrote: *"The hardest trial of my husband's life was parting with his mother. Such partings were the only occasions when I ever saw him lose entire control of himself... She had been an invalid for many years... parting seemed to her the final one. Her groans and sobs were heart rendering. She clung to him every step when he started to go...The general would rush out of the house, sobbing like a child, and then throw himself into the carriage beside me, completely unnerved... At the first stop he was out... buying fresh fruit to send back... Before we were even unpacked...he had dashed off a letter."* [4]

Hard work in the farm fields and stints at horse shoeing honed and developed the adolescent who boasted there wasn't a horse in Harrison County he couldn't ride or shod.

By the time he was age ten, Autie's sister Ann had married an attorney named David Reed and was living in Monroe. When she became pregnant for her first child Marie, overtures were made for his visit and eventual move north this time enrolling in New Dublin School.

Monroe was a small town, yet divided by social class even to the extent that Uncle George who ran a local livery where Armstrong worked had little contact with the more prominent citizens of the town. A celebrity in his own right, Uncle George

had patented an affordable horse shoe he dubbed "Goodenough."

Enduring friendships began when Autie enrolled in Alfred Stebbins' Academy where he shared a desk with John Bulkley. Bulkley remembered how he carved the initials "A. C." into the desk top yet always insisted on using his full name, *"I want people to know who I am."* [25]

One such recognition occurred at his first encounter with Elizabeth Clift Bacon. The blond haired schoolboy was a mere six blocks from his sister's house when the chestnut haired impetuous "Libbie" Bacon as she was known called out to him.

"Hello you Custer Boy!"

Before he could stop and respond she had disappeared into the ostentatious home of her father Judge Daniel S. Bacon of Monroe, Michigan. [28]

For the next few years both would pursue different paths. The Custers primarily Democrats and Methodists had little contact with the social conscience Bacons who attended the Presbyterian Church and were staunch Republicans.

Custer at age sixteen returned to Ohio and entered the McNeely Normal School, later called Hopedale Normal College, it was the first co-educational college for teachers in eastern Ohio. While attending Hopedale, Custer, together with classmate William Enos Emery, paid for their room and board by carrying coal. Custer graduated from McNeely Normal School in 1856 and taught school in Hopedale and "District Five" school house in Cadiz, Ohio. Despite his parents encouragement to return home Armstrong remarked *"I never intend to make my living by working on a farm."* [22]

His first month's salary as a school teacher was $26 which he brought to his mother and poured into her lap.[25]

In a letter to his father Armstrong wrote *"...You and Mother instilled into me principles of industry, self-reliance, honesty. You taught me the value of temperate habits, the difference between right and wrong. I look back on the days spent under the home-roof as a period of pure happiness, I feel thankful for such noble parents."* [29]

As a young school teacher, Autie was barely older than the students he taught. He was as much a rambunctious playmate as when they occasionally locked him out of the school house or when he would play familiar songs for them on an old accordion.

Armstrong now a full time school teacher, had taken up board with the Alexander Holland family. The family's young daughter Mary Jane, whom he referred to as "Mollie" was as smitten as the "Bachelor Boy," a name he referred to himself in intimate letters he wrote her. When the romance heated up and they were discovered rendezvousing

in the trundle bed, Custer was asked to leave and forbidden to return.

Word around town was, that a boy from Jefferson County had failed his pre-exams at West Point. This left a vacancy that Armstrong was determined to fill. Humble beginnings would not prevent him from trying to wrangle an appointment to the Citadel along the Hudson River. Even though his representative was a Republican, the Democratic Custer sought his appointment in a bold letter addressed to Congressman John H. Bingham.

"Sir: Wishing to learn something in relation to the matter of appointment of cadets to the West Point Military Academy, I have taken the liberty of addressing you on the subject...I remain, Yours respectfully G. A. Custer"

Congressman Bingham was quite impressed by the letter, but his appointment may have had a lot more to do with Alexander Holland's attempt to get him out of the district as his young daughter Mary had come of age and he knew full well that a cadet couldn't marry until graduation five years away. In parting for New York Autie left a poem for his "Mollie."

To Mary
I've seen and kissed that crimson lip
with honied smiles o'erflowing.
Enchanted Watched the opening rose
Upon thy soft cheek glowing.
Dear Mary, thy eyes may prove less blue,
Thy beauty fade tomorrow,
But Oh, my heart can ne'er forget
Thy parting look of sorrow.

First known photograph of G. A. Custer courtesy of Custer Battlefield Museum Garryowen, Montana.

WEST POINT:
THROUGH TRIALS TO TRIUMPHS

"*My career as a cadet had but little to commend it to the study of those who came after me, unless as an example to be avoided.*"[30]

Military enlistment had promised $28 dollars a month for five years while getting a good education to boot.[34]

Trading his plowshare for a sword, as a Plebe, the lowest form of life according to West Point Tradition, he rated a canvas home on the Plain called "Beast Barracks." Hazing became a way of life for those misfortunate under classmen. But the cadets soon came to know and respect the humor of Custer who they nicknamed "Fanny" for the length of his hair and fairness of his complexion.

His long hair soon garnered him demerit. His solution and remedy being to shave his head bald! Another demerit soon followed *"Hair out of uniform"* for which he wore a wig until his locks grew back. And to keep his unruly curls under control he lathered them down with scented hair oil earning the name "Cinnamon." More flattering he observed than Fanny.

This system of demerits called "Skins" sometimes trumped the Plebes' standing in class. One Hundred demerits during a semester earned immediate expulsion from the Academy. Armstrong ran close to ninety eight at any given time during a semester. He spent sixty six consecutive Saturdays walking guard duty to shave some of those skins from his record. Most were earned for: *"Swinging arms while marching"* when he wasn't "Late at Parade" or "Throwing bread" when "Throwing snowballs" wasn't available.

To a large degree he was the most popular man on campus. When he wasn't in trouble or skirting trouble, he was leading his class in athletics and horsemanship. He was frequently the center of the storm for what mischief that was going on.

Finally when assigned to the "2nd Division Company D South Barracks" he shared quarters with Jim Parker from North Carolina and Tom Rosser and John Pelham from Texas and Virginia respectively.

They became inseparable and the culprits of most pranks being pulled and bestowed on their fellow classmates. Often the case they made their marks not only in class, where Armstrong asked his instructor to say "Class Dismissed" in Spanish and when the instructor complied Cinnamon stood up and led the assembly out of the room; but also in Buttermilk Falls where Benny Haven's famous drinking establishment was often frequented although strictly off limits to Cadets and Plebes of the Academy.

Since the allure of Buttermilk Pancakes, female companions and Whiskey Flips would guarantee immediate expulsion, the cadets would often sit back to back to drink their intoxicants and honor bound

Custer's first furlough photograph.

they would confess to never observing their fellow classmate indulge in such provocations. This exclusive club became known as the West Point Protective Association and like ancient orders before, these bonds held true through four years of conflicts when states divided.[1]

At the end of their first two years the cadets were afforded leave. Many returned home, some did not return to the academy. Autie wrote to Ann, *"I would not leave this place for any amount of money, for I'd rather have a good education and no money than a fortune and be ignorant..."*

Exams at the Academy were a daily occurrence and after hours of drill and instruction the cadets would stay up into the early morning hours boning up on the next day tests. *"We study incessantly. I and others only average about four hours' sleep in the twenty-four. I work until one at night. And get up at five. All my classmates are becoming pale and thin. We do not complain. On the contrary, everyone is anxious and willing."* Burning the midnight oil often earned Armstrong demerits for "Lights on after hours."

To remedy this unfair disadvantage a scheme was hatched to steal Professor Church's Mathematical Test from his room while he slept. Best laid plans of mice and men are sometimes brought to roost especially when Lieutenant Douglas' cock decides to crow. Armstrong tore the page from Church's exam book and made a hasty flight through the second story window. Landing unscathed he vowed to cook the chicken's goose. And sure if he didn't, with his roommates partaking of this delectable course while Cadet Officers later discovered unidentifiable bones in the boodle box inside the fireplace. No one confessed to the absence of Douglas' prize rooster, but Armstrong earned some skins for *"cooking utensils in the chimney."* [32]

Armstrong's love and appreciation for good music was reflected in his constant and insistent urgings to have Elias Andruss strum and play "GarryOwen" on his small guitar.[33] Yet when politics flared, and Abraham Lincoln became candidate for the newly formed "Republican Party," Tom Rosser led the Southern students in a rousting chorus of "Dixie" while it was Fanny who encouraged his classmates to stand during the playing of the National Air "The Star Spangled Banner." His devotion to God and Country and fidelity to the flag allowed that he became credited with starting that tradition long before it became our National Anthem.

"It is useless to hope the coming struggle will be bloodless or of short duration. Much blood will be spilled and thousands of lives, at least, lost. If it is to be my lot to fall in the service of my country and my country's rights I will have no regrets." Should he fall in battle, Armstrong expressed his wish to be buried at West Point Military Academy.

As each class had the opportunity to design their own ring for graduation Autie's class of May 1862 chose "Through Trials to Triumphs" as their motto. For one cadet it would be almost prophetic.

In November the country elected the Rail Splitter President. And as each successive Southern Cadet resigned his commission Autie, who was as usual walking guard duty, came to an abrupt halt and presented arms as they departed at the south docks.

When the first shots of the Civil War were fired at Fort Sumter Armstrong's class was graduated a year early. His course of study being cut short by one year in order to supply the Federals the much needed officer corps. While Patrick Henry O'Rourke led the June Class of 1861 in academic standing; it was for Armstrong to bring up the rear. Graduating thirty four in a class of thirty four, and christened "The Immortal." Ordinarily, such a showing would be a ticket to an obscure posting and mundane career, but he had the fortune to graduate just as the war caused the army to experience a sudden need for new officers. His tenure at the Academy was rocky, and he had come close to expulsion in each of his four years due to excessive demerits, (812 just 23 shy of expulsion) many (453 offenses), for pulling pranks on fellow cadets.[34]

Assigned as Officer of the Guard while awaiting orders, Autie was patrolling beast barracks when he

Custer is thought to be standing over the left wheel.
West Point Special Collections & Archives USMC Library.

Graduation Photograph. June, 1861.

Custer in New York. July, 1861.

happened upon Peter Ryerson and William Ludlow who had come to blows over the water pump. Other Plebes had tried to separate the two combatants until Armstrong shouted, *"Stand back boys, let's have a fair fight."* All at once Lieutenants William Hazen and William Merrill appeared and had him arrested. He was charged with starting a riot and brought before a Court Martial. If not for the Commandant of Cadets, John Reynolds his career in the military would have come to an abrupt end, before it began. Just as "Custer's Luck" had drawn his appointment to the Academy, it was about to shuffle the deck on his dismissal of the court martial charges.

West Point. The Library

CIVIL WAR
GLORIOUS WAR

Probably no period of our country's history was as greatly influential in shaping our present day lives as that of the American Civil War. Our greater moral awareness, laws, customs, military warfare applications and innovations in medicine were a direct result of that bitter conflict. It was a romantic time in our country's history not quite a hundred years old yet we were questioning some of our values. Those values would eventually split the nation in four long years of bloody conflict, threatening to tear apart and destroy the very fibers of our democracy.

A war that shaped our National Character, as well, as forged and "touched by fire" an individual's heroism. Although graduating last in his class at West Point, George Armstrong Custer went on to become the youngest Major General in the history of our country's Military.

Hastening toward Washington, Armstrong stopped off briefly in New York City at Horstmanns of Philadelphia, to purchase his first uniform as a Commissioned second lieutenant and by late evening he was prowling around the Capital in search of the Adjutant General's office. On the steps of the capitol building he ran across Congressman Bingham who asked, how he might like to meet his Commander in Chief?

Brought before General Winfield Scott, hero of the Mexican War and overall commander of the Union Army he was given an unprecedented inter-

Portrait of Joseph Fought.

view and drew the assignment of delivering dispatches to the front. The only hitch being the commandeering of a horse. After spending the better part of the next day visiting all the stables and liveries in the city Armstrong was resigned that there were no horses in Washington. Seems most of the Capital's citizenry had procured all of the carriages, buggies and buckboards along with all the four footed equines for a large picnic planned just outside Manassas, Virginia, where the first major conflict of the war was to take place.

Disheartened and forlorn, Custer was about to give up when a mounted soldier appeared leading a horse.

Joseph Fought, who would serve as his Bugler/Orderly through the rest of the war, had been assigned to procure remounts and was leading a gelding that Armstrong immediately recognized. "Wellington" had been the horse he'd ridden and come within a hairsbreadth of besting Hiram Ulysses Grant's record jump at the Academy. Convincing Fought to wait a bit while he collected the dispatches allowed "Custer's Luck" to prevail.

Riding all night they joined up with Company G 2nd U.S. Cavalry at 4:00 AM on the morning of July 21 near a farm owned by Wilbur McClean, just outside Manassas, Virginia.

2nd Lieutenant G. A. Custer with Lieutenant James Washington, a confederate prisoner but Custer's friend and classmate at West Point.
May 20, 1862.

By now General Irwin McDowell was confidently assigning his lieutenants their positions on the field of battle. Many thought the war would be of short duration. The President, Abraham Lincoln had called for 75,000 ninety day volunteers. At the time most feared the First Battle of Bull Run, might be the first and last battle of the Civil War.

During the engaging salvos and cannon barrage a great cheer emoted from the picnickers. But as the fog of battle lifted, realization of the proximity of conflict caused confusion and immediate evacuation by both civilian and military alike. A long string of transports and union troops intermingled and made a hasty retreat towards Washington.

The debacle called "The Great Skedaddle" found the Army of the Potomac in low morale until word arrived that General George B. McClellan would be taking overall command. During the next few months the Army found its identity and George Armstrong Custer along with it developed as a soldier.

2ⁿᵈ Lieutenant G. A. Custer joins General Winfield Scott Hancock and staff in a portion of Julian Scott's painting. Smithsonian Institute, Washington DC.

'Intrepid Balloon'. May 1862.
Peninsula Campaign.

Custer's assignments in Virginia saw him on a variety of Staffs and virtually participating in every engagement of the Army of the Potomac with the exception of Fredericksburg and Chancellorsville. Throughout the next year he was shuffled from Kearny to Hancock, and because of his West Point training was eventually assigned to gun emplacements around Fortress Monroe. Although officially part of the reconstituted 5th U.S. Cavalry, with which he served through the early days of the Peninsula Campaign in 1862, he spent little time in the saddle.

Build up of Confederate forces around the Capital required accurate intelligence and President Lincoln ordered the formation of the U. S. Balloon Corps. Professor Thaddeus Sobieski Constantine Lowe headed up this selective branch of seven balloons and an untold number of aeronauts who were placed under the Corps of Topographic Engineers.

In choosing a military aviator, Lowe had settled on General Fitz-John Porter who eventually made over 100 ascents. His most hair raising occurred at 5:00 AM on April 11, 1862. Inspired by a thirst for information, Porter disregarded the usual precautions and ascended over 900 feet before the lone tether line snapped from vitriol having been carelessly spilled, thus weakening the securing rope.

Detached from the grounding tether and climbing skyward, Porter's balloon took to free flying before veering toward the enemy emplacements. *"Open the valve,"* the ground crews shouted. Keeping a cool head he carefully jotted down positions and details while Confederate snipers continually fired at him in hopes of bringing down the great monster. Suddenly a counter current of air captured the balloon and sent it hurling back to the Union line. Managing to open the valve, Porter soon found himself hurling toward the ground before striking a shelter tent not 100 rods from General McClellan's headquarters.

The commotion was enough to change policy. McClellan felt his general officers least suited for flight, while second lieutenants were quite expendable. So with great reluctance, fresh blood was brought into the corps. Custer bored with construction duty landed the assignment with the Balloon Corps and became one of the country's first Aeronauts.

"Previous to this time I had never even examined a balloon except from a distance," wrote Custer in his "War Memoirs." *"(Asked) whether I desired to go up alone, my desire, if frankly expressed, would have been not to go up at all."*

His reaction was typical given the fact that the balloons were filled with hydrogen and highly flammable. Although none of Lowe's balloons were ever shot down by enemy fire, it was common knowledge that a few of Lowe's predecessors had ascended to the heavens in fiery chariots.

The success of the corps outweighed its unacceptance as it was passed from the Military Telegraph Corps to the Quartermasters Department then on to the Corps of Engineers. The Confederates considered the Corps a nuisance at best and limited troop movements whenever one was aloft. But imitation proved the sincerest form of flattery when the South called for the ultimate sacrifice-ladies' silk petticoats-in making their own military balloon.

The patchwork ship of various hues made its debut during the Seven Days Campaign of 1862. Since their only access to gas was from sulfuric acid and iron filings from a factory in Richmond, the balloon was inflated there and sent by railroad to ascend where desired. Later, transported by steamer down the James River, the petticoat balloon made ascensions near the Union occupied lines. But the Confederate Balloon Corps was to be short lived when the steamer ran aground and was captured by the Federals.

For Lieutenant Custer, Aeronaut duty held little honor but gave great consternation. Proving resourceful and innovative; he suggested rather than mid-day observations; early morning reconnaissance would provide a glimpse when the enemy

Custer wading the Chickahominy.

was starting breakfast fires. His dawn ascensions aboard the hot air balloon, "Intrepid" garnered him recognition when he observed Confederate forces withdrawing from positions around Yorktown and eventually relieving the pressure on Washington, D.C.

This discovery afforded him a reprieve and reassignment to dirty duty on General Barnard's staff eventually putting Armstrong back in the saddle during the pursuit of Confederate General Joseph E. Johnston up the Peninsula. on May 22, 1862 when Gen. Barnard and his staff were reconnoitering a potential crossing point on the Chickahominy River, they halted and began making calculated estimates of its depth. Custer overheard his commander mutter to himself, *"I wish I knew how deep it was?"* Without haste Custer sprang from his horse, plunged in and waded out to the middle of the river. *"That's how deep it is, General!"*

To the astonishment of the officers and staff, Custer then crossed to the other side and with his notebook made extensive drawings of the enemies' camp and positions. General Barnard and staff wasted little time returning to the Army of the Potomac Headquarters and relaying the vital information to General McClellan.

So impressed was the Union Commander that he authorized the young Lieutenant to lead an immediate attack with four companies of the 4th Michigan Infantry crossing the Chickahominy River just above New Bridge. The attack was successful, resulting in the capture of 50 Confederates and seizing the colors of the 5th Louisiana "Tiger Zouaves;" the first Confederate battle flag of the war. Maj. Gen. George B. McClellan, commander of the Army of the Potomac, termed it a *"very gallant affair,"* congratulated Custer personally, and brought him onto his staff as an aide-de-camp with the temporary rank of captain.[35] Later General McClellan remembered their meeting and how Armstrong had put little

Captain G. A. Custer.

Original portrait of Custer made by Prince de Joinville. Courtesy of American Heritage Archives.

General George B. McClellan with staff & dignitaries (from left to right): Gen. George W. Morell, Lt. Col. A.V. Colburn, Gen. McClellan, Lt. Col. N.B. Sweitzer, Prince de Joinville (son of King Louis Phillippe of France), and on the very right - the prince's nephew, Count de Paris. Fall 1861.

importance on what he had accomplished, *"a reckless, gallant boy, undeterred by fatigue, unconscious of fear and with a head that was always clear in danger."* Custer became known for clear and intelligible reports of what he observed under the heaviest of fire.[36]

That same mutual admiration was expressed by the young newly appointed captain, *"I've more confidence in General McClellan than in any man living. I would forsake everything and follow him to the ends of the earth... Why, I'd lay down my life for him... With McClellan to lead us we know no such word as fail."*

Worshipped by his men, McClellan made certain they were fully fed and fully paid. He demanded and received the best in arms and equipment. They were well trained and well clothed. *"No General could ask for greater love and more unfounded confidence than he received from his men."*

In March of '62 while preparing for the Peninsula Campaign he wrote: *"Soldiers of the Army of the Potomac, I know I can trust you to save our Country. Ever bear in mind that my faith is linked to yours. I am to watch over you as a parent over his children. And you know that your general loves you from the depths of his heart."*

McClellan was found everywhere amongst his 'Boys' and everywhere he was received with unbound enthusiasm. Through his own initiative he developed the 'McClellan Saddle' an Army standard that would endure for over a century! George McClellan was responsible for the Bayonet and Drill Manuals translated from the French and instructed to our troops in the wars to follow. He introduced the shelter or 'Pup Tent' that became the standard issue to all U. S. Troops.

Drilling and preparing the troops consumed a tremendous amount of time. The energy that

'Little Mac' put into the task wore on him and the strain often did not make for good diplomacy with the President and his cabinet. Accused of snubbing the President and inaction prompted the President to write: *'I think the time is near when you must either attack Richmond or give up the job and come to the defense of Washington. Let me hear from you instantly.'*

Lincoln's plan of Emancipation for the Slaves and capture of Richmond was at odds with McClellan's strategy. The Young Napoleon as the press came to call him wanted to conquer and defeat the Confederate Army sure and completely. To free the slaves was secondary if at all considered. He hoped to win the war with as few causalities as possible. Over 618,000 men would eventually perish by war's end. *"I view with infinite dread any policy which tends to make this contest simply a useless effusion of blood."*

By the time the Seven Days Battle had ended Autie had seen the Elephant and exclaimed, *"War Glorious War."* Having shot his first opponent and captured his horse and equipment. *"The saddle, which I also retain, is a splendid one covered with black morocco and ornamented with silver nails."* But it was the captured sabre that became his prize possession. It was a straight Toledo Blade and much like Excalibur it was claimed Armstrong was the only man who could wield it. *"No me saques sin razón: no me envaines sin honor: Draw me not without provocation, sheath me not without honor"* was emblazed on the blade and this became his own battle cry. The failure of the Peninsula Campaign resulted in McClellan's removal and replacement by General John Pope in early August of '62. Armstrong drew furlough to Monroe and caused quite a stir when the dapper fair-haired Soldier Boy made appearances at the Humphrey House in downtown Monroe.

Judge and Elizabeth C. Bacon.
Payette Collection Monroe Evening News.

Judge Daniel S. Bacon was as interested as anyone to hear fresh reports from the front and often had conversations with the celebrity captain. His reputation as a ladies' man soon developed; Fannie Fifield numbered herself amongst his conquests and boasted as much to the Judge's daughter.

Frequenting some of the drinking establishments was a favorite past time for soldiers on leave, and Armstrong Custer was never one to do things half measure. On one of his sporting sprees he stayed a little longer than he should have. Quite inebriated, he soon realized the most difficult time navigating home to his sister's house. Falling down he became sick in front of the Bacon house while the Judge and Libbie observed him from a front window. This wasn't good for his reputation or his future relationships with the Bacons. Sister Ann met him at the front door and with the "Good Book" ushered him into the parlor for some instruction. Although from that day on he never touched a drop of alcohol for the rest of his life, this single indiscretion proved to be the biggest hurdle to overcome as he attempted to impress Judge Bacon and win the hand of his only daughter.

Custer & McClellan with Lincoln. Custer is at extreme right of the photo.

Autie as a dashing captain.

Libbie's Graduation Photo. June 1862.

Meanwhile, Pope's defeat at Second Bull Run saw the reinstatement of General McClellan to Command.

Within a month the Army of the Potomac engaged the Confederate Army under General Robert E. Lee in what was to become the bloodiest day of the war. Twenty-Three Hundred Union troops lay dead on the field near Antietam Creek. It was said a person could walk the entire battlefield from one side to the other on the bodies of soldiers without having to touch the ground.

Ten days after the battle McClellan wrote the President: *"This Army is not now in condition to undertake another campaign nor bring on another battle."* One out of every four men who had marched into battle were dead, wounded or missing.

Once again President Lincoln insisted if he wasn't going to use the Army of the Potomac to let Lincoln borrow it; finally relieving McClellan and eventually replacing him with General "Fighting Joe" Hooker. Little more than a flash in the pan, Hooker is best remembered for his camp followers christened "Hooker's Women."

While on leave to Monroe in November of 1862, Armstrong received a formal invitation to a party held at the Boyd Academy where Libbie had graduated the June before as Valedictorian of her class.

Conway Noble, had triumphantly won the honor of escorting Libbie that evening but somehow had botched the whole affair and looked to his old school chum to bail him out. Guest of Honor, recently promoted Armstrong Custer replete in his Captain's uniform approached Libbie for the introduction and was amazed at the beauty of Monroe's prettiest sweetheart.

"I understand your promotions have been quite rapid?" Became her first declaration.

"I've been most fortunate." Was his reply and most fortunate was the situation for him, duly smitten his "Custer's Luck" would come into extreme play and all his talents would be drawn upon to win this fair lady's hand.[37]

Remembrance of Autie's drinking spree provoked Judge Bacon to forbid contact between the young couple. Custer not to be unhorsed showed up at numerous occasions even positioning himself strategically in the best pew of the Presbyterian Church the one that best observed Libbie during the worship service.

Through a mutual friend Annette Humphrey the couple began a flirting courtship that respected the Judge's admonition but dangerously fueled the flames of a storybook romance.[15]

So madly in love was he with Libbie Bacon; that even his military sash proclaimed his affection, embroidered with her initials "L. C. B." which he told everyone stood for "Light Cavalry Brigade."[38]

Upon his return to the front Armstrong learned McClellan had once again been relieved of command and he now reverted to the rank of first lieutenant.

'Custer at Aldie'.

Joseph Fought his orderly was assigned elsewhere and told, *"You're not with Custer now, so cut your hair!"* Shortly thereafter Custer fell into the orbit of Maj. Gen. Alfred Pleasanton, who was commanding a cavalry division. The general was Custer's introduction to the world of extravagant uniforms and political maneuvering, and the young lieutenant became his protégé', serving on Pleasanton's staff while continuing his assignment with his regiment. Custer was quoted as saying that *"no father could love his son more than General Pleasanton loves me."* After the Battle of Chancellorsville, Pleasanton became the commander of the entire Cavalry Corps of the Army of the Potomac and his first assignment was to reorganize the Union Cavalry and to locate the army of Robert E. Lee, moving north through the Blue Ridge Mountains. Fought with unshorn locks was now back with Armstrong and continued his association for the duration of the war.

Custer distinguished himself by fearless, aggressive actions in some of the numerous cavalry engagements that started off this campaign. Brandy Station and Aldie two northern cavalry victories brought Custer to the attention to his superiors. And then on June 28, 1863, three days prior to the Battle of Gettysburg, General Pleasanton promoted Elon Farnsworth, Wesley Merritt and George Armstrong Custer from the ranks of lieutenant to brigadier general of volunteers. Custer, now nicknamed "The Boy General" lost no time implanting his aggressive character on the "Michigan Cavalry Brigade." Designated the Second Brigade of the 3rd Cavalry Division and until now unprecedented "The Michigan Cavalry Brigade" was made up exclusively of men all from the same state. The 1st Michigan Cavalry, the veteran

Boy General at 23.

'Custer at Hanover'. By Artist Don Gallon. Image courtesy of Gallon Historical Art. www.gallon.com

unit had seen action almost immediately at the beginning of the war and gained a reputation as a Sabre Regiment. Within two years the 1ˢᵗ Michigan was thrown together with the 5ᵗʰ, 6ᵗʰ and 7ᵗʰ Michigan Cavalry Regiments to form the Michigan Cavalry Brigade. Under the command of General Joseph T. Copeland, the Brigade saw action in small skirmishes, but was unable to show their mettle in battle because the Union high command was still reluctant to use cavalry as an effective force. Regulated to escort and courier duty they were eager for their "coming out."

Arriving on the scene wearing gilt spurs, tall boots and a personally designed and outrageous black velveteen uniform, George Armstrong Custer could only be described as a *"circus rider gone mad!"* hardly officer material or so they thought. The twenty-three year old, only two years out of West Point was about to change all that!

On the morning of June 30, 1863 the Michigan Cavalry Brigade pitched into Rebel forces under Major General JEB Stuart near Hanover, Pennsylvania. The outcome of the battle was little more than a nose tweaking to Stuart's Black Horse Cavalry, but the Brigade had experienced the "Boy General's" prowess under fire. Custer's style often claimed to be reckless or foolhardy, bore a larger degree of military planning and was always the basis of every Custer "dash." Marguerite Merrington explained in "The Custer Story," that George Custer *"meticulously scouted every battlefield, gauged the*

enemies weak points and strengths, ascertained the best line of attack and only after he was satisfied led the 'Custer Dash' with a Michigan yell focused with complete surprise on the enemy in routing them every time." Custer's own mark and reputation as an aggressive cavalry brigade commander willing to take personal risks by leading his Michigan Brigade into battle, was remembered by Joseph Fought his Bugler, *"All the other officers were exceedingly jealous of him. Not one of them but would have thrown a stone in his way to make him lose prestige. He was way ahead of them as a soldier, and that made them angry."* [39] One of them being his Division Commander General Judson Kilpatrick. Kilpatrick, who's ruthless disregard for his men's and horses' welfare had earned him the reputation and title "Kill Cavalry" was in direct contrast to Custer's concern for his men. James Kidd of the Michigan Cavalry Brigade defended his old commander at the Statue Dedication in Monroe years later, *"He was not a reckless commander. He was not regardless of human life. No man could have been more careful of the lives of his men."* [40]

Yet it was do or die near Hunterstown, Pennsylvania on July 2, when one single Brigade of Union Cavalry and Battery "M" of 2ⁿᵈ U. S. Artillery under Captain Alexander Pennington found themselves in an awkward position trying to hold back an entire Confederate Division under General Wade Hampton. Putting out skirmishers and backing them with cannon, Custer instructed Captain Thompson, of A Company, 6ᵗʰ Michigan to make

Norvell Churchill.

stay and fight. At the precise moment Stuart's cannons fired four distinct volleys signaling Lee his own division was in place. Custer immediately instructed Pennington to unlimber his guns and soon after one of the luckiest shots of the war occurred when a cannon ball struck a Rebel gun squarely down the muzzle rupturing and knocking it off its carriage.[41] The contest at East Cavalry Field, lasted well into the afternoon hours capping off Lee's unsuccessful penetration of Cemetery Ridge. Charges, counter charges and hand-to-hand combat ensued. Drawing the Toledo Blade from its scabbard, Custer rode out front of the troops and led a mounted charge of the 1ˢᵗ Michigan Cavalry, *"Come On You Wolverines!"* breaking the back of the Confederate assault. Custer's brigade lost 257 men at Gettysburg, the highest loss of any Union cavalry brigade.

General George Meade down played the encounter on East Cavalry Field, reporting the battle as "indecisive" but Custer's report of August 22 boasted, *"I challenge the annals of warfare to produce a more brilliant or successful charge of cavalry..."* Of Churchill the report stated, *"I desire to commend to favorable notice Norvell Churchill, Company L, 1ˢᵗ Michigan..."* Churchill's "remarkable gallantry" earned him the appointment as one of Custer's special orderlies and the care of the General's mounts became Churchill's responsibility until Custer left the Michigan Cavalry Brigade to

ready for a charge. *"I'll lead you this time, boys. Come on!"* Cried Custer as he cantered up the road. In the excitement of the moment twenty-three year old Norvell Churchill broke loose from his regiment and joined the mad dash, sabre slashing.

Sixty men slammed into more than six hundred. A death-raking volley brought Custer's horse down. Just as a Confederate officer lunged forward to thrust a sword through the Golden Cavalier, a quick reflexive action by Norvell Churchill saved Custer's life. As Churchill rode in, he deflected the Rebel's sabre blow with his own sword, and then shot the Confederate officer point blank with his revolver. Shoving out his hand to the general, Custer leaped onto the croup of Churchill's saddle and the two rode out of harm's way.

One of Custer's finest hours in the Civil War occurred the next day just east of Gettysburg. In conjunction with Pickett's Charge to the west, Robert E. Lee dispatched Stuart's cavalry on a mission into the rear of the Union Army. En route to Little Round Top, Custer encountered the Union cavalry division of Brig. Gen. David McMurtie Gregg, directly in the path of Stuart's horsemen. Convinced that the Michigan Brigade could make a difference, Gregg asked him to

Custer snatched up his guidon after his color bearer was shot at Five Forks in 1865 By C. Gómez.

General Custer Leading the Wolverines at Gettysburg by Franklin Briscoe 1889. (Liberty Heritage Society Museum).

head up the 3rd Cavalry Division. By the end of the Gettysburg Campaign Custer had had seven horses shot from under him, but Norvell's son Hugh, remembers his father saying *"Custer's horses had the reputation for being the best fed in the cavalry".*

As a small boy, Custer had been raised in the hills of southeastern Ohio. His father was a blacksmith and relied on the young boy's knowledge and help with horses. This early upbringing proved an advantage when the motion of mounted fury thundered across the sweeping countryside Custer was in front of the attacking column. In the galaxy of generals, only a few would stand out like the rising Morning Star of Venus. The swallow tailed ensign they would follow was constructed in the field. Custer's personal colors (one of five designating flags) were carried throughout the Civil War. His last flag perishing with him at the Little Big Horn. The flag was first made of red over blue wool cut in a swallowtail configuration with white hospital bandages cut in the shape of sabres and crossed in the middle of the Guidon. Each kept the same color and design. And each proved to be the largest guidon in the Union Army, carried on a nine foot staff when regulation called for an eight foot flag pole. Like his flashy uniforms, he wanted his men to have little doubt where he was on the battlefield; which was usually in front of the charging troops.

Over the next few months young men between the ages of 18 to 30 would follow this Boy General, the Murat of the Union Cavalry shedding their blood on the battlefields of Monterey Pass, Falling Waters and Boonsboro places that once echoed and reverberated, "Through Trials to Triumphs," but are now all but completely lost in our nation's conscience.

'Brigadier General G.A. Custer'.
Army of the Potomac. 1863-1864.
By C. Gómez.

Generals Custer & Pleasanton.

Paid $13.00 per month, soldiers in blue endured fears of death from battlefield wounds and infections from unsanitary conditions in camp. Subsisting on a meager diet of beans, coffee, bacon and hardtack. The hard bread measured 3 $^{1/8}$ by 2 $^{7/8}$ inches and was 1/2 inch thick; issued in quantities of nine squares to a soldier per day. During hard times rations were cut 1/3 deriving the familiar saying, *"three squares a day."*

Those volunteers under the guide of Custer soon became the élan of the Union Army and a threat to the Confederate Cavalry under their best horseman, J.E.B. Stuart.

It had been almost a year since Autie had been socially introduced to her and Libbie, though not initially impressed with him, now looked forward to his return to Monroe. Her father, had disapproved of Custer for being the son of a blacksmith and the thought of his young daughter in widow weeds was now a larger discouragement.

Custer's rise to fame in the Military had but few rivals as he had become the youngest Brigadier General in the Union Army. Judge Bacon could hardly pick up the papers and not read of the "Boy General with the Golden Lock's" most recent exploit. The press loved him and so did his "Wolverines." Their unflinching loyalty and patriotism saw them courting danger in the vanguard of the Union juggernaut. Defeating Stuart's Black Horse Cavalry at Gettysburg was just the beginning. For Custer, rank did not dilute his prowess in battle. One of his greatest attributes during the Civil War was what Custer wrote of as "luck" and he needed it to survive some of these charges.

Eleven horses were shot from under him in over sixty successful cavalry charges. His men swore by him and were willing to follow him into the breath of the enemy's cannon. And follow him they did, accumulating more causalities than any other cavalry unit during the war. That sacrifice was not without gain. Vicious frontal assaults and daring flanking attacks captured more battle flags, cannon and prisoners than any other command. He won them over with his readiness to lead attacks (a contrast to the many officers who would hang back, hoping to avoid being hit); his men began wearing elements of his uniform, especially the flowing red tie he wore around his neck; it became the trademark of the units he led. Men under him soon adopted the distinguishing badge of honor tearing their own red underwear into cravats and earning the nickname of the "Red Tie Boys."

But whatever his success on the battlefield, his most intimate friends knew there was but one dark haired young lady in Monroe that he pursued with as much fervor as any cavalry charge upon the field of battle. His proposal to Libbie Bacon, was pure Custer in cunning and style. Donning his Full Dress Gray Cadet Uniform on bent knee he proposed to her in the fall of 1863.[38]

"The very thought of marriage makes me tremble. Girls have so much fun." She implored him to wait at least a year.[31]

The worst thing about loving a soldier," wrote Libbie," *is that he is as likely to die as to live... and how should I feel if my soldier should die before I have gratified his heart's desire?"* [42]

His adversaries on the battlefield knew him by sight and admired and respected him as a worthy warrior, while a special crack unit of Texas Rangers had but one assignment: "Kill Custer." Despite their attempts he came through the War relatively unscathed but for shrapnel wound to his left leg that killed the horse he was riding at Culpepper Court House.

First reports in the paper spoke of the Boy General's death in a charge at Culpepper; but later retractions of the story, to Libbie's relief and jubilation, announced Autie's flesh wound and fifteen day leave to Monroe.

"I'm yours forever and ever," was her response to his announcement to be married at once. Her only hesitation was to break the news to her father the Judge.

Custer who had been fearless in combat now floundered before the strictness of her father and it was for Libbie to boldly announce, *"Armstrong and I are engaged to be married."*

The Judge although at first against it finally acquiesced. Armstrong's victory having gained the approval of Judge Bacon and was able to marry her, fourteen months after they had first formally met. On Tuesday, February 9, 1864 the day before Lent, all of Monroe prepared for the Wedding of the Century. Victorian superstitions claimed a Tuesday wedding bode well for good health.[43]

Judge Daniel Stanton Bacon promised himself he would not cry during what would be *"The most splendid Wedding ever seen in the State of Michigan."*[44]

Cold weather bundled guests began arriving at the First Presbyterian Church long before the appointed hour. Shortly before six o'clock the church was filled to almost suffocation,[45] equipped with old-style box pews[46] every seat was taken by the more than 200 participants who appropriated the gallery and vestibule for standing room only.[47]

Autie's parents and siblings were seated upfront. They now owned a home in Monroe purchased by the Boy General in hopes Maggie could graduate from Boyd Academy as his wife to be had done two years before.

Reverend Erasmus J. Boyd, Principal of the Young Ladies Seminary, where Libbie graduated, assisted by Reverend Dr. Charles N. Mattoon, were to perform the traditional marriage service.[48]

Promptly at 8:00 PM the organist Mrs. Minnie St. John Loranger,[49] piped up the wedding march and the Bridesmaids entered on the east aisle led off by Ann Darrah and Marie Miller dressed in white tarlatan, with gauze veils, just reaching their shoulders.[15] Autie's groomsmen Conway Noble and John Bulkley, who had been Custer's desk mate at Stebbin's Academy, made their way down the west side of the pews. Annette Humphrey, Libbie's best girlfriend was her maid of honor, she followed next down the

Capt. Jacob Greene & Annette Humphrey.

east side as her beau Captain Jacob Greene, who was Armstrong's Best Man, would later go on to head one of the nation's largest insurance companies[50] sauntered down the west aisle in full dress uniform.

The Groom in Brigadier-General dress frock and sash appeared next with uncharacteristic shorn locks, escorting the Bride's stepmother Rhoda Pitts Bacon down the west aisle to the altar.[24]

At the appropriate notes *"Here Comes the Bride"* on the organ everyone stood as Libbie leaning on her father's arm, *"won all hearts"* [44] in her rich white silk dress[37] with long sleeves, wide at the wrists, narrow at the shoulders, and crossed with horizontal stripes, and fashionable pyramid effect[51] becoming bertha of point lace and a long train.[37]

The Bride wore her chestnut- brown hair parted in the middle and rolled above each ear, and coiled in a knot down the back of her slender neck[51] covered by a long veil with a crown of orange blossoms worn above the brow. She carried a bouquet of red roses, which matched her own rosy cheeks, tied with white silk.[52] About her throat she wore a broach containing a lock of her mother's hair.[51]

As tradition dictated she wore short white gloves with a slit in the finger so she would not have to remove them for the ring to be placed. *"Something old, something new, something borrowed, something*

blue, and a lucky sixpence in your shoe." Her shoes were flat, decorated with bows on the instep and she had a lace handkerchief with her maiden initials in blue script.[53]

As soon as their vows were exchanged, Reverend Boyd turned to the congregation and pronounced them, *"Man and Wife."* The wedded couple turned to face the congregation, *"Whom therefore God hath joined together, let no man put asunder."*

Reverend Mattoon pronounced the Blessing, *"The Lord bless you and keep you; The Lord make His face to shine upon you and be gracious unto you:*

The Lord lift up His countenance upon you and give you peace:

Both now and in the life everlasting. Amen."

The Married Couple paused a moment, then walked out without looking left or right, exiting the church where a crowd of well wishers applauded, cheered and threw rice and birdseed as they climbed aboard a sleigh drawn by four white horses that whisk them off to the Bacon Home for a formal reception.

In the formal parlor decorated in white with orange blossoms the wedding party received their guests. Showering them with congratulations over three hundred towns folk and relatives squeezed past the Judge and Libbie's stepmother Rhoda, Autie's parents, Nettie Humphrey, The Bride and Groom and their attendants. Autie was quite attentive to Libbie and never left her side.[43] Displayed in the same small room for all to see was the silver dinner service from the 1st Vermont Cavalry consisting of a Grecian Pattern six-piece tea set (tea pot, coffee pot, water urn, sugar bowl creamer, and slop bowl all engraved "Custer"). Along with a cake basket, castor, pair of salt dishes, berry spoon and a pitcher with waiter and two goblets. The pitcher inscribed, *"Presented to the Bride of Brig. Gen. G. A. Custer by the Officers of the 1st Vermont Cavalry Feb. 9th, 1864."* [54] The 7th Michigan Cavalry also presented the couple a companion seven piece silver tea service. There were berry spoons, a wedding spoon engraved: *"Libbie C. Bacon, Feb. 9th, 1864"* a silver card case, silver salver calling card receiver, gold lined thimble napkin rings, syrup cup, sugar spoons, two white silk fans, Mrs. Elizabeth Barrett Browning's published poems "Whisper to a Bride," in a lavishly bound edition, a knit breakfast shawl, a mosaic chess stand of marble, a handsome Bible from Judge Bacon and a white parasol with black lace from Libbie's step mother. Autie's gift to Libbie was a gold hunting case watch with her new initials "E. B. C." on the outside.[43]

Guests partook of three wedding cakes, one elaborate cake, and two smaller ones for the bride and groom.

The larger, a rich, fruit cake was decorated with white frosting and orange blossoms.[53] Libbie's smaller white cake was cut and the first piece set aside for a later anniversary. The groom's cake was much darker and a small thin piece was given to the guests as they departed at 10:00 PM.

As soon as the cakes were cut Libbie and her Bridesmaids disappeared upstairs where they helped her to change into her brown traveling dress. From her wedding bouquet she gave each of her bridesmaids a red rose. At midnight the entire wedding party boarded a train in Monroe bound for Cleveland.[37]

It was an un-restful evening for Judge Bacon as he stayed awake all night for fear of burglars stealing the wedding gifts, which he packed up and took to the bank the next morning.[55]

By 9 o'clock the next morning the train pulled into the Cleveland depot and that afternoon a fine reception was held for the couple by Charles Noble.[55]

A brief stop in Buffalo was followed by attending "Uncle Tom's Cabin" in Rochester and a visit with Aunt Charity in Onondaga, New York.

Everyone was excited to see Libbie's elaborate trousseau, and she was equally excited to show it off. Each dress was carefully unpacked and held up for examination. Autie again had to endure the chorus of *"Oohs and Aahs."*

Along with her white merino opera cloak with silk hood and rich tassel she next displayed her breakfast dress of light blue merino with basque and sleeves scalloped and bound with black velvet. A double dress of lilac silk faced and trimmed with plaid was held up followed by a light green silk with narrow stripes, trimmed with lace and bugle ornaments. Everyone liked the hotel sacque with black buttons, the black velvet circle dress and dark green velvet riding habit with military brass buttons and galloons (This almost a match to the Boy General's own Black Velveteen.) A dark brown traveling dress of empress cloth with white buttons, a lavender velvet dress hat and a waterproof with arm holes rounded out the fashion show.[56]

All at once the porter came for their baggage as the train was about to leave the station. Autie grabbed everything and began stuffing willy nilly expressing more vigor than experience he soon found himself entangled in the hoop undergarments.

"Surrender!" Came the whoops and shouts of the relatives. All followed to the station and as the car receded into the distance they could still make out the Boy General waving his large sombrero, losing his golden hat cords in the merriment.[37]

A re-union with Uncle Den and Aunt Eliza at Howlett Hill was followed by a precarious sleigh ride across the frozen Hudson River to the General's alma mater: West Point Military Academy. The instructors

Brigadier General G. A. Custer with his bride Elizabeth (Libbie) Custer. February 1864. By Mathew Brady & Co.

may not have been excited to see him, but the dogs remembered him and were glad for his return.

The young cadets adored Libbie and some of the old professors welcomed her by claiming the privilege of kissing the bride.

Armstrong was not amused and sulked, *"Well, you left me with them, Autie!"* [15]

All too soon their leave was over and the two headed to Virginia to the theater of war. Not to be left behind, Libbie found her first home and traditional carry across the threshold at Pony Mountain, a carriage pulled by white horses and a fairy tale life and adventures as the only woman to ride with the Army of the Potomac for the duration of the war.

In May, when the cavalry corps of the Army of the Potomac was reorganized under Maj. Gen. Philip Sheridan , Custer took part in the various actions of the cavalry including the Battle of the 'Wilderness' and Yellow Tavern, where Jeb Stuart was mortally wounded by John Huff a soldier in the Michigan Cavalry Brigade. Little Phil's confidence in Custer, allowed him to continue to lead his "Wolverines" throughout the Shenandoah Campaign. On June 11 Sheridan's plan included a dual Federal movement against Trevilian Station, where Custer was humiliated by having his division pinned between two

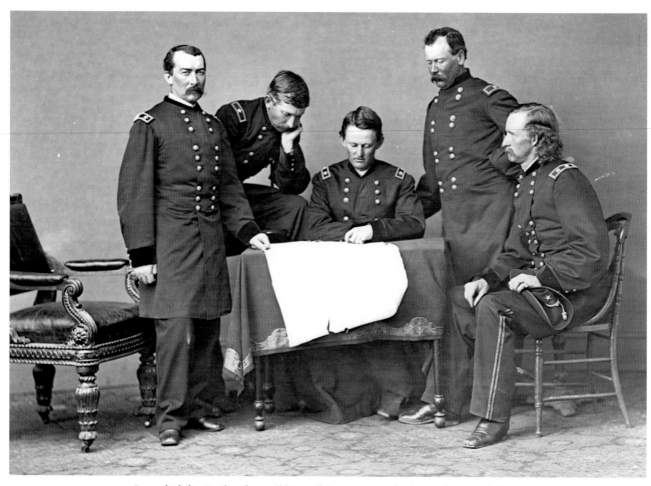

General Philip H. Sheridan and his staff, January 3, 1865, by Mathew Brady & Co.
From left are: Generals Sheridan, James Forsyth, Wesley Merrit, Thomas C. Devin, and George A. Custer.

crack Confederate Divisions, one of which was led by his old West Point classmate Thomas L. Rosser. The 28 year old Texan had managed to arm most of his troops with captured Spencer repeaters making him an even match for the Boy General.

Rosser's approach was concealed by the heavy growth of trees and underbrush that had brought Fanny's column to a standstill. Six Confederate Cannon were moved into position atop a large knoll overlooking Trevilian Station. Before Autie could react Confederate Major Roger Chew opened up with his cannon and Rosser blazed away with his cavalry. Hardly having time to realize the lay of the land Armstrong and his staff became surrounded. *"From the nature of the ground and the character of the attacks that were made upon me our lines resembled very nearly a circle... no place could be called under cover."* [57]

'Trevilian Station. Cavalry Battle'.
By James E. Taylor 1881.
(LBHNM)

Pivoting the fifth and sixth as skirmishers and directing Pennington to unlimber his guns Armstrong dismounted, threw off his jacket and rolled up his sleeves. It was Root Hog or Die. Firing back with his revolver The Boy General was determined to make a stand.

Numerous charges by Wade Hampton's Cavalry Corps were repulsed. Refusing the line when both Fitz and Rooney Lee hammered the Wolverines from all sides. At one point over running Battery M's field pieces. Armstrong, Pennington and 30 Red Tie Boys were not to let 'em have 'em, taking all the guns back before retiring to their tri-angle defense.[44]

All at once a shot cracked next to the Boy General; Color Sergeant Mitchell Bellior spun around, *"General they've killed me! Take the flag."*

The silk swallow tail guidon made from Libbie's silk pantaloons was torn from the staff and shoved into Armstrong's tunic. *"Boys there's a few gentlemen between us and home. I'm going home, who wants to follow?"* Mounting the Brigade and drawing his Toledo Blade he began plunging and slashing a hole through the Confederate line.

Over 41 Wolverines lay dead on the field, 242 captured; all the wagon trains overrun and his personal baggage now in enemy hands. Armstrong's personal cook Eliza Brown and her carriage managed to break free and rejoin the Boy General who lamented they captured everything *"...except my toothbrush!"*[39]

Both Autie and Libbie chagrined at the capture and printing of their love letters in the Richmond papers, *"I don't care if fifty rebels read this letter."* She wrote him, *"I miss your kisses!"*[15]

Of the dozen or more top Generals of the Civil War, one can hardly forget mentioning George Armstrong Custer. He was highly prolific in an age of mass bloodshed and modern warfare, standing out like a relic from the classics of old. A knight errant in manners and decorum riding to the front to bow to his opponents before instructing his bandmaster Major Charles Axtell, of the 5th Michigan Regimental Band to strike up "Yankee Doodle" and in a flash plunge across the field. It was this controversial nature that attracted so much attention. Admired by the public and his superior officers, yet at the same time scorned for his youth and appearance on the battlefield. General Sheridan claimed, *"Custer was the only man who never failed me."* Promotion to Major General at twenty five saw his transfer to the Third Cavalry Division, causing the men from the Michigan Brigade to petition to be transferred with him or be given an old pair of his boots to inspire them in combat.

Custer, now commanding the 3rd Division, sought permission to have his kid brother Tom transferred to his staff. Despite his parents objections, Tom had entered the 21st Ohio Infantry and had served at one point as a body guard to General U. S. Grant. The brothers became inseparable, *"He should have been the General and I the Captain"*

"Grant and his Generals". By Ole Peter Hansen Balling. Custer is painted at extreme left of the print.
National Portrait Gallery, Smithsonian Institution; gift of Mrs. Harry Newton Blue in memory of her husband
Harry Newton Blue (1893-1925), who served as an officer of the Regular U.S. Army 1917-1925.

Ken Hendricksen

'General George Armstrong Custer'. By Ken Hendricksen.

Drawing of Custer Bowing to Rosser.
From Whittaker's Complete Life of Custer 1876.

Major General G. A. Custer with Libbie and
Lieutenant Thomas Ward Custer,
January 1865. Mathew Brady & Co.

wrote Autie when Tom became the first man in history to receive two Medals of Honor within four days of each award for captured Confederate battle flags.

Sheridan now declared "Total War" on the Shenandoah Valley, first defeating Rosser's Command at Tom's Brook known as "Woodstock Races." Upon capturing Rosser's baggage train this time, Armstrong, in a letter to Rosser thanked him for the new Gray frock coat but cautioned the tall Texan to have his tailor to cut the coattails a little shorter next time.[58]

That same coat saved Autie's life when the Confederates over ran the farm at Lacy Springs where he was staying and he donned the coat and

'Sheridan's Final Charge at Winchester'. By Thure de Thulstrup.

instructed a confederate aide to saddle his horse allowing him to escape through enemy's lines unharmed.

When Confederate Lieutenant General Jubal A. Early moved down the Shenandoah Valley and threatened Washington, D.C., Custer's division now all affecting the "Red Tie" was mobilized and dispatched along with Sheridan to the Valley Campaigns of 1864. They pursued the Confederates at Third Winchester and effectively destroyed Early's army during Sheridan's counterattack at Cedar Creek. Custer and Sheridan, having defeated Early, returned to the main Union Army lines at the Siege of Petersburg, where they spent the winter.

The Holidays proved a joyous time for the Custers and their close family and friends when Libbie spent Christmas at Elmwood and Armstrong accepted Jesus Christ as his Savior. From then on he would take "A knee" to pray before going into every battle.

General Thomas L. Rosser.

Major General G. A. Custer and staff at the Elmwood mansion, Winchester, Virginia, December 25, 1864. By William H. Bowlsby.

General Custer presenting captured battle-flags at the War Department, Washington, October 23, 1864. Engraving published in Harper's Wekly, November 12, 1864.

In April 1865 the Confederate lines were finally broken and Robert E. Lee began his retreat to Appomattox Court House, pursued by the Union cavalry.

Custer distinguished himself by his actions at Waynesboro, Dinwiddie Court House, and Five Forks where Tom Rosser was entertaining the Rebel Generals at a shad bake when the camp was overrun with Union soldiers.

By war's end Custer's men had captured 111 pieces of field artillery, 10,000 prisoners (7 of which were general officers) and 65 battle flags while in the process never losing a gun or their own colors.

Between 1861 and 1865 618,000 Americans would lose their lives fighting for beliefs and causes that pitted brother against brother. Those 600,000 causalities averaged out to 423 deaths for each day of our Civil War. Seven Thousand Union Soldiers alone would perish in less than half an hour in 1864 when Grant ordered his forces to storm Confederate defenses at Cold Harbor.

"On Fame's Eternal Camping Ground Their Silent Tents are Spread; And Glory Guards With Solemn Round the Bivouac of the Dead" [59]

With the hasty withdrawal from Petersburg, Lee attempted a link up with General Johnston in the Carolinas. While a swift break out to the west was thwarted at Sayler's Creek. A third of the Confederate Army including seven General Officers and over nine thousand Confederate troops surrendered to Ole Curley. When South Carolina's Artillery Battalion was captured, Frank Huger, one of Armstrong's old classmates from West Point was

'Custer Accepting Flag of Truce'. By A. R. Waud from Whittaker's Popular Life of Custer.

'Surrender at Appomattox'. By Thomas Lovell.

brought before him. Still wearing the famous Mexican spurs once owned by Santa Anna who'd worn them at the siege of the Alamo, Armstrong

From a M. Brady photo May 23, '65 wearing the Santa Anna Spurs.

suggested they roll dice for the possession of the spurs. Ever after Huger claimed the Boy General carried loaded dice.[44]

After successfully blocking Lee's retreat, capturing 25 cannon and four locomotives loaded with 24,000 rations it was inevitable to Custer, that the flag of truce was presented when Robert E. Lee sought an audience with Ulysses S. Grant to tender his surrender at Appomattox Court House on April 9, 1865. What started in the back yard of his farm was now to end in his parlor; Wilbur McClean's table upon which the surrender was signed was presented to Armstrong as a gift for his wife by General Sheridan, who included a note *"There is scarcely an individual in our service who has contributed more to bring about the successful conclusion of this war."*

"A Country with no regard for its past will have little worth remembering in the future." Abraham Lincoln wrote of those trying years of war. Within days the nation in shock and utter sorrow, learned of President Lincoln's assassination.

Summoned to Washington the Third Cavalry Division encamped outside the city in preparation for the Grand Review. General Sheridan having been ordered to Texas asked that Custer lead the entire Cavalry Corps on May 23rd. Unbeknownst to Armstrong his officers had gone into the city the night before and purchased every bit of red cotton, silk and felt fabric they could get their hands on. It was claimed there wasn't a full union suit in all the city of Washington! From this fabric was fashioned "Red Ties" for the entire Cavalry Corps to wear in honor of the Boy General. The next morning groomsman Johnny

Mrs. Carrie Farnham Lyon and Major General George A. Custer, October 18, 1865, at Hempstead, Texas.

Cisco brushed, tacked and saddled Don Juan, a large 16 hands bay thoroughbred, who had been captured in the last stages of the War. He was the son of the triple crown winner, Glencoe, who'd had his best showing at Belmont, Preakness and the Kentucky Derby. Custer assumed his position at the front of the procession that swung off Constitutional Avenue onto Pennsylvania Avenue amidst the cheers and shouts of the citizenry. All at once about fifty young girls all dressed in White ran forward and began pelting the men with flowers. They took up a common cheer, *"Custer! Custer! Custer!"* One young lady attempted to throw a large wreath about Don Juan's neck. Falling short Custer drew out his Toledo Blade *"Draw me not without provocation, sheath me not without honor"* and tried to catch it on the point of the blade. The loud *"Shinniinnggg!"* made by the removal of the sword from his scabbard caused Don Juan's ears to draw back and as if at the starting gate he took the snaffle bit in his teeth and bolted forward. The wind caught Custer's wide brimmed slouch hat sailing it into the air behind him, while Don Juan bounded past the Reviewing Stand before Armstrong could render the proper salute to the President, Generals Grant and Meade and all the other dignitaries in Washington. Gathering a tight rein and managing to get Don Juan under control,

Custer returned to his place in the procession and rendering the proper honors as he made his second pass before President Johnson. After two days of review the Headlines in the Press read: Custer steals the show!

Mrs. Elizabeth B. Custer and Major General George A. Custer. October 18, 1865, at Hempstead, Texas.

'Staghounds'.
By Frederic Remington.

Just as suddenly Custer boarded a train and left for the South en route to Texas. Confederate General Kirby Smith unwilling to capitulate and Mexico rotting with its own internal difficulties, Texas became the tinderbox of national security. Inroads of diplomacy with Emperor Maximilian might prevent a war with France but American interest in Texas was at stake.

Leaving the train at Louisville and embarking on a Mississippi steamboat called the Ruth, the landscape passed by in a kaleidoscope of ruined and burned out homes devastated by the war, sorrowful faces and looks that spoke of hopelessness. From New Orleans, Custer and his staff disembarked and by horse crossed to Alexandria where troops of the First Iowa, Second Wisconsin, Seventh Indiana, Fifth and Twelfth Illinois Cavalries reluctantly awaited their arrival. Regiments disinclined to soldier since most of the Army had been disbanded and sent home created difficulties and several cases of mutiny plagued the early stages of the route westward. It was Autie's hope that they would eventually form a cohesive unit and work in tandem with a desire to reconstruct the beleaguered States.

On the march Libbie was able to master the feat of dressing in 7 minutes so as not to delay the Cavalry's progress. But one hurried occasion she left her famous green riding habit from her trousseau in a pine grove. By day she bounced along the trails to the accompaniment of the horses puffing and neighing, the soldiers' voices cheery in the constant changes of weather. When the first Northerner struck Father Custer, who had been assigned Forage Master, found himself buried within his tent while Libbie tried desperately not to cower. Only Autie stayed calm until the rain and wind abated.

Their arrival in Texas after days of arduous travel, brought great excitement! Bivouacking at the Groce Plantation, previously a Prisoner of War Camp brought a heavy hearted feeling, but it became

apparent that much of the welcome was actually due to the Boy General's conduct towards the local residents. As a friend and protector he was very respectful of everyone, never did he treat the people as though they had just lost a major war. Their appreciation later expressed thirty-three days after the Battle of the Little Big Horn, when the Texas Legislature passed a Joint Resolution sent to the United States Congress, expressing condolence to the families and declaring how Custer had endeared himself to the people of their great state.

The planters often would seek out the General and invite him to go hunting. Arriving early in the morning with their packs of hounds, sometimes numbering thirty to forty baying and howling until their master blew on a polished Texan steer hunting horn. Armstrong was soon to acquire a horn of his own as each plantation gifted him several hounds at the end of each hunt. Byron and Ginnie were amongst the first of his acquisition each greyhound having a personality of its own. Ginnie became Libbie's favorite and Byron was a one man dog, often positioning himself between Autie and Libbie in their bed and attempting to extract Libbie by pushing heavily against her back with his paws. The animals became an almost unconscious substitute for the children they were unsuccessful in having. Throughout the rest of their lives together the dogs played an important role. Each gave unrequited love. As if in competition with the planters Armstrong added Scotch hounds, stag hounds, wolf hounds and beagles to his menagerie.

On December 27, Custer still wearing the Mexican spurs that had once belonged to General Antonio López de Santa Anna, visited the Alamo, the site of Texas' Birth of Freedom. One of his biggest regrets was Sam Houston passing several years before.

Through the generosity of then Gov. Hamilton and later Gov. Throckmorton, the staff moved to Austin and were allowed to live in the Blind Asylum.

It was to become General Custer's Headquarters throughout the rest of his stay. How truly delightful life became for Autie and Libbie while living in this two story stone building by renowned architect Abner Cook!

But it was the children that held their dearest memories. Each day Armstrong would ride out and visit the School for the Deaf, he was both friend and student to their sign language. Something that in later years would hold his stead in council with the Great Chiefs.

On February 1, 1866, Custer was mustered out of the volunteer service and returned to his permanent rank of captain in the regular army, assigned again to the 5th U.S. Cavalry. Custer applied for and took an extended leave, exploring options in New York City, where he considered careers in railroads and mining.

Following the death of his father-in-law in May 1866, Custer returned to Monroe, Michigan, where he considered running for Congress and took part in public discussion over the treatment of the American South in the aftermath of the Civil War, advocating a policy of moderation. He was named as the head of the Soldiers and Sailors Union, which was regarded as a response to the hyper-partisan Grand Army of the Republic, also formed in 1866, and headed up by Republican activist John Alexander Logan.

In September 1866 Custer accompanied President Andrew Johnson as a Presidential body guard on a journey by train known as the "Swing Around the Circle" to build up public support for Johnson's policies towards the South *"With malice towards none and charity for all."* During the junket Mexican Minister to the United States, Matias Romero, offered a position as adjutant general of the army of Benito Juarez of Mexico, who was then in a struggle with the self-proclaimed Maximilian I (a foil of French Emperor Napoleon III), Custer requested a year's leave of absence from the U.S. Army, but his appointment was blocked by U.S. Secretary of State William H. Seward, who feared offending France.[60] Custer also denied a charge by the newspapers that Johnson had promised him a colonel's commission in return for his support, though Custer had written to Johnson some weeks before seeking such a commission. Custer and his wife Libbie stayed with the President during most of the duration of the trip, at one point physically confronting a small group of men in New Market, Ohio who repeatedly jeered Johnson, causing Armstrong to remark *"I was born but two miles from here, but I am ashamed of you."*

On July 29, 1866 Custer was appointed lieutenant colonel of the newly created U.S. 7th Cavalry Regiment, headquartered at Fort Riley, Kansas. As a result of a plea by his patron, General Philip H. Sheridan, Custer was appointed and approved to the brevet rank of major general. This guaranteed Libbie would receive the pension of this higher rank should he fall in combat.

Autie and Libbie lounge on the steps of Custer's headquarters in Austin, Texas, with family and friends, November 1865.

THE SEVENTH CAVALRY

The Frontier Army often times put down and criticized for their thankless efforts in pacifying the plains in the later part of the 1800's, to this day remains the scapegoat for the Government policy. Whether right or wrong that policy fomented an insatiable appetite we once termed Manifest Destiny. Those individuals who had a strong sense of patriotism and sense of duty served our nation during the bitter struggle known as the American Civil War, later saw duty on the prairies. Theirs was the awesome undertaking of policing 2.5 million square miles with but 25,000 troops. Certainly a let down from the millions of troops thrown into the conflict between 1861-1865. From their initiation to the American plains to their first encounter with the American Indian, each soldier had to learn and adapt their skills and knowledge in dealing with a society so diametrically opposite to the military training they had been taught at West Point; principally using the modern European tactics. And as our Government changed policies the Army had to

change with it. The overall tedium and boring duty coupled with the liberal press that promoted the image of a brutal military presence in occupied lands.

The American Indian whose way of life became threatened even prior to the introduction of the white man to this continent became accelerated with the alliances and greed for hunting lands previously owned or lorded over by fiercer tribes.

This was a society that by 1866 realized 270,000 people from 125 distinct Indian groups (they were outnumbered 10 to 1 by the immigrants already homesteading on the plains) pivoting on the verge of extinction. With the coming of the railroads more immigrants ranging into the hundreds of thousands were soon to join them. This would impact the 13 million buffalo that up to then had sustained the Indian tribes.

'Cavalry Charge on the Southern Plains'.
By Frederic Remington.

To police them Secretary of War Edwin M Stanton settled for an Army of 50,000 soldiers. July 28, 1866 established the *"Act to increase and fix the Military Peace Establishment of the United States"*. The law increased the regular Cavalry from six to ten regiments and the regular Infantry from nineteen to forty-five regiments. The Artillery remained at five. But by 1874 the total troop force was cut to 27,000.

This group was responsible for carrying out the policies set in Washington D.C. Whether they were the correct policies remains the question for historians and scholars to ponder.

The Frontier Officers' Corps was composed of former regulars who'd held higher rank during the Civil War in a volunteer militia but now due to the downsizing remained on government salary at a lesser rank. Eight point eight percent of the officers were civilians appointed as officers from the Civil War. Seven per cent were West Point graduates. The rest had attained officer status from time served in the enlistment ranks.

By 1874, thirty percent of the officers had been commissioned from the ranks, half of these were foreign born. Between the Civil War and end of the century forty two percent of the officers had received their commissions within two years following the war, although they may not have received another promotion by the system of seniority that made attaining a higher rank long and tedious.[61] Custer himself, would have achieved full colonel had he survived one month longer in 1876, with William Emory's retirement he was next in line of seniority and would have received his first promotion in ten years.[62]

The government reeling from the economic collapse of '73, made every effort to conserve the military budget. In some cases the enlisted man went months before receiving the promised pay. Although the bulk of the recruits had previously

Custer's headquarters flag.
Courtesy of Louis Pfeiffer.

hailed from Ireland, Italy or Germany they were joined by a cross section of America, representing soldiers of fortune, ne'er do wells, thieves, renegades and deserters from both the Union and Confederate ranks. Most historical accounts were written by the well educated officers; the enlisted man, whether American born or immigrant was usually illiterate, their life upon entering the military regulated to unconditional servitude, and at the mercy of inexperienced junior officers who placed their lives in constant jeopardy. Homesick, disease ridden men between the ages of 17 to 35 soldiered on in extreme weather conditions, far removed from the comforts of eastern civilization. For a paltry $13.00 a month they tolerated sadistic, mean-tempered non-commissioned officers who subjected them to brutal punishment and harsh duty where the only complaints could be made through chain of command. Not surprising was the temptation of the Gold Fields that lured the men to "French Leave" and found some regiments depleted as much as twenty five to forty percent from desertion alone.

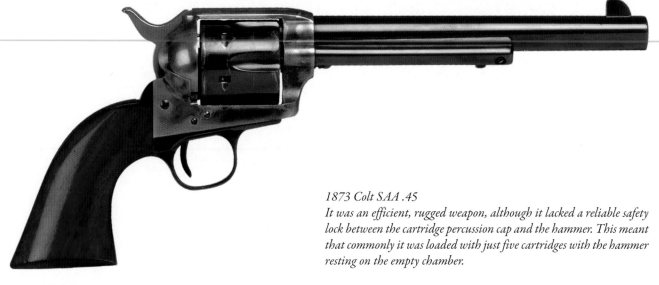

1873 Colt SAA .45
It was an efficient, rugged weapon, although it lacked a reliable safety lock between the cartridge percussion cap and the hammer. This meant that commonly it was loaded with just five cartridges with the hammer resting on the empty chamber.

From October of 1866 to October of 1867 the Seventh Cavalry lost over 512 men to desertion, carrying off stolen property and provisions from the command.[63] The Adjutant General's report of 1876 gave a total of 4,606 deserters in the Army over a previous three year period.[64] Sheridan had little tolerance and ordered that deserters were to be shot on sight.

Most troopers stood five feet four inches and weighed between 120 to 180 pounds. A steady diet of dried beef, sliced pork and hardtack allowed the issue uniform to never go out of style or become uncomfortably tight on a growing boy.

'Cavalry types in 1876 at the time of Little Big Horn Battle'. By C. Gómez.

Enlisted 1872-pattern campaign hat.

Guard duty and punishment detail was furnished to those who'd stayed longer at the hog ranches and drinking establishments off post. Discipline was as severe as having one's head shaved or being bucked and gagged. Flogging had been outlawed but deserters in time of war chanced an execution squad. For those more fortunate, stoking the commanding officer's fireplaces got them out of the barracks that could have doubled for a meat cooler.[65]

The equipment furnished him was often times obsolete and antiquated with provisions left over from the Civil War. Clothing met the minimal needs and requirements. The standard shirt was a loose-fitting, light-gray pull over with three metal or bone buttons. Civilian blue or the popular "hickory" or checkered shirt were purchased from the meager salary not garnished for laundress or sutler bills. Often the enlisted man owed gambling debts to non-coms or other enlisted men in the company. *"Pay would be taken out in blood and then the doctors work their cures, and tinker up our bruises."* [33]

Uniforms of inferior material called "Shoddy" were ill fitting at best and often fell to pieces after a good soaking in the rain. When uniform standards changed in 1872 it was several years before regula-tions were enforced and even then a great deal of latitude was permitted in the field. Four button sack coats surplus from the war saw extensive wear on campaign as the regulation five button coat was retained for garrison duty. Trousers provided in standard kersey (sky blue in color)often times made it to remote posts without the reinforced seats and crotch for the cavalry, coming only in Infantry style that required canvas or flour bag material to be sewn in by the company tailors. Most issue were too small or too large. Suspenders or white woven cotton braces were non existing although the trousers came with buttons to accommodate those lucky enough to purchase a wide variety sold at the post trader stores. Considered an undergarment, Victorian etiquette required they be covered by a vest at minimum.

Officers often wore buckskin trousers or jackets. These required the use of suspenders from the skins stretching and fluctuation of weight during long and arduous campaign.

Head gear came in a variety of shapes and sizes. The 1859 forage or "Bummer" cap lasted into the '70s and were replaced by the '72 forage cap, but still as a matter of choice, Kepis were worn in a

Enlisted 1872-pattern forage cap.

number of variations that had survived the Civil War and were preferred by some.

Standard issue was the Andrews black slouch hat; a bizarre wool concoction that could be rigged up to present a Napoleonic appearance until caught in a rain storm and then effecting more of an elephant ear look to those unlucky enough to have to retain it. Civilian purchases of silver belly, black or tan slouch joined the popular straw or "boater" that was worn by officers and enlisted alike.[66]

Troop "K" known as the "Dudes" adopted and refashioned the white canvas pants and stable frock coat, for field wear; tight fitting and trimmed in imitation fringe.[67]

Standardized uniforms came much later. In 1872 dress uniform specifications were changed reflecting and influenced to a large degree by the Franco-Prussian War. Where the French had carried a style most emulated by the Civil War Armies; by both Union and Confederate, the torch was now passed to the British and Germanic look. Each branch of the service used their designating color piping on the blouse, cords and flourishes. An immediate distinc-

tion was the adding of the helmet to the issued head gear. Where once kepis and chapeaus dominated the look, helmets now were vogue in formal and proper military dress.[68] Field dress still reflected a more casual adherence to these regulations.

Just as Napoleon had done, Custer separated his companies by the color of their mounts. "A" Troop rode Blacks, "B" "D" "H" "I" and "L" had Bays. Troops "C" "G" and "K" all rode Sorrels. "E" was the Grey Horse Troop and "F" rode Chestnuts. The Regimental Band rode White horses and often the Trumpeters had Whites or Greys. "M" Troop was made up of the bulk remaining, all mixed.[69]

Custer's initiation to the frontier came when he took part in Maj. Gen. Winfield Scott Hancock's unsuccessful expedition against the Cheyenne in 1867. On June 26th, 1867 Lt. Lyman Kidder's party made up of ten troopers and one scout were massacred while en route to deliver dispatches to Custer from Gen. William Sherman. Attacked by a party of Sioux and Cheyenne, Custer discovered the remains of Kidder's patrol days later; all were stripped, scalped and mutilated.

Army clothing regulations. 7th Cavalry Dress Uniforms. 1882.

NCO Full Dress.   *Captain Full Dress.*   *Stable Frock.*

Period illustration showing Custer staring at Kidder's cavalrymen corpses heavily mutilated by the indians.

When a cholera epidemic swept the plains of Kansas, Armstrong's career took a brief detour. Court-martialed at Fort Leavenworth, Kansas for being AWOL after abandoning his command in the field to seek out his wife, whom he thought might have been exposed to the plague, he was arrested, tried and sentenced to one year suspension without rank or pay. His return to duty in 1868, following 10 months of forced leave, was at the request of Maj. Gen. Philip Sheridan, who wanted Custer for his planned winter campaign against the Cheyenne.

"General Sherman, Sully and myself and nearly all the officers of your Regiment have asked for you, and I hope the application will be successful. Can you come at once? Eleven companies of your Regiment will move about the first of October against the Hostile Indians from Medicine Lodge Creek towards the Wichita Mountains." [70]

Predatory bands of Arapaho, Cheyenne, Comanche, Dakota and Kiowa had raided settlements along the Kansas-Colorado Borders between August and November 1868. Over 600 horses, mules and almost 1,000 cattle were stolen; 157 settlers were ruthlessly murdered and scalped; 57 wounded and 20 women and children captured and outraged.

Upon Sheridan's orders, Custer established Camp Supply in the heart of Indian Territory the early part of November 1868. It would serve as a supply base for the winter campaign. Lieutenant W. W. Cooke put together 40 of the best shots in the Regiment who were exempt from regular duty and made up the elite marksmen of the Seventh.

"Yesterday my twelve Osage guides joined me, and they are a splendid-looking set of warriors, headed by one of their chiefs called "Little Beaver." They are painted and dressed for the war-path, and well armed with Springfield breech-loading guns. All are superb horsemen. We mounted them on good horses, and to show us how they can ride and shoot, they took a stick of ordinary cord-wood, threw it on the ground, and then, mounted on their green, untried horses, they rode a full speed and fired at the stick of wood as they flew by, and every shot struck the target." [6]

Sheridan first had reservations about a Winter Campaign.

Lieutenant Colonel G. A. Custer with his Osage Indian scouts, Fort Dodge, Kansas, November 1868.
Note Custer's headquarters flag flies above the pelican.

General Philip H. Sheridan.

"Nonsense Phil, we can move they can't." "Well, Custer," he said, *"You're the only man who never failed me."*

During a heavy blizzard the command left Camp Supply on the morning of the twenty third to the regiment band tunes of "The Girl I Left Behind Me." There was over a foot of snow on the ground, the temperature extreme. This was to be a Seventh Cavalry operation. The Red Ties who had been with the Boy General during the war-still sported the familiar cravat, and now eagerly they rode to the chase.

Custer and his men storming Black Kettle's Village on the Washita River.

'Custer's Demand'
By Charles Shreyvoguel.

The snow continued to come down in a constant white out; navigating the trail became almost impossible. How could they make war against an enemy they could not see? "Ouchess" the name given to Armstrong by his Osage Scouts, pulled a compass from the pocket of his buffalo coat and set a bearing toward Wolf Creek.

The orders from Sheridan were plain and simple *"You will proceed South, in the direction of the Antelope Hills, thence towards the Washita River, the supposed winter seat of the hostile tribes; you are to destroy their village and ponies, kill or hang all warriors, and bring back all women and children."*

Suddenly word came from Jack Corbin, one of the civilian scouts, Major Joel Elliott had broke the hostiles' trail. A war party, evidently the last of the season, one hundred fifty strong, leading due South. Disgusted with the cold weather they were going home.

Stripping the command for rapid transit they cut loose the wagon train and pushed forward with all haste. From here on campfires were not allowed, for fear they would discover the column's movements. Orders prohibited a word above a whisper. Soon the guides halted, *"Me smell smoke"* one of the Osage exclaimed. And then in the twilight hours on the morning of November 27, 1868, the sound of a baby's cry. Custer had found Black Kettle's Cheyenne stronghold on the Washita. By the light of the Morning Star he could see the smoke curls form a mist above the sleeping wigwams. The Osage scouts prepared for battle as the frozen strains of "Garryowen" signaled the attack.

Met by a barrage of gunfire and swirling arrows, the troops opened fire with their Spencer Repeating Carbines; those same weapons that had turned the tide of battle during the Civil War. But this was not Gettysburg. This enemy proved to be more complex. This would be their first real battle, with the Children of the Sun.

Amidst the screams of horses, wounded moaned and gave up the ghost. Before long the providence of death dwelt in the ashen faces and burned out lodges along the Washita River. Blucher the General's favorite hound lay dead in the snow full of arrows. Tom had received a wound to the hand.

Lieutenants Hamilton, Elliott and 19 enlisted men were killed. Over 103 warriors lay dead, fifty-three Indian Women and Children secured and captured. Eight hundred and seventy five ponies put to death. One thousand one hundred buffalo robes, 500 lbs of powder, 1,000 lbs of lead and 4,000 arrows had been destroyed. This was regarded as the first substantial US. victory in the Southern Plains War, thus effectively crippling and helping to force a significant portion of the Southern Cheyenne onto a U.S. appointed reservation. Now it was for Custer to meet with Stone Forehead in the Lodge of the Medicine Arrow Keeper. Like an apparition he and Lieutenant William W. Cooke appeared on the plain before their village.[71]

There was a trilling by the Indian Women as "Hiestzi" the name they had given to the Yellow Hair Chief, tight reined his horse into the surround of canvas and buffalo hide lodges. Each moment a heart beat from death. A bare foot walk on the blade of a skinning knife. Though the countenance of his face did not betray it, there was an ache in the pit of his stomach.

"It is for two white women, Sarah White and Annabelle Morgan captured six months before on the Kansas border, that I have come" Yellow Hair signs to Stone Forehead.

They were among 28 women and children captured and carried off by Dog Soldier raiding parties since 1866.

To win their release will squelch the reprisals on both sides and end this bitter war. Beneath the scared bundle Armstrong sat before the elders of the Southern Cheyenne.

Each express their grievance and scorn for the pony soldier. It is not that they feared the Yellow Hair, but rather the might of the Seventh Cavalry. For that day, in the Lodge of the Medicine Arrow Keeper the pipe is passed, a promise made; Hiestzi will never again make war on the Cheyenne. A curse on him if he does. And they anoint his troop boots with pipe dottle and ash. It is murmured the two women shall go free.

During the long winter campaign allegations surfaced by Captain Frederick Benteen, chief of scouts Ben Clark, and Cheyenne oral tradition that Armstrong had taken a Cheyenne wife. Unofficially 'married' to Monaseetah, daughter of the Cheyenne chief Little Rock (killed in the Washita battle), who gave birth to a child in January 1869, two months after the Washita battle. Cheyenne oral history also relates how she bore a second child, fathered by Custer, in the fall of '69. Monaseetah was later kept with the command as an interpreter and emissary, convincing the rest of the Cheyenne, Arapahoe and Kiowa to come into the reservations. The command traveled 1,295 miles[72] during the late winter and early spring, when supplies ran short, it was Root Hog or Die, *"Custer fed us on one hardtack a day and "The Arkansas Traveler." complained a trooper."* [51]

It is not for the number of Indian lives that were lost during the Staked Plains Campaign, but for those who were spared that Custer became known as the Foremost Indian Fighter on the Plains.

Lieutenant Colonel G. A. Custer, February 9, 1868 at Fort Still, Wichita Mountains.

FLAGS AND INSIGNIA

1. Commissioned Officers (COs)
The commissioned officers wore shoulder-straps piped with the yellow of the cavalry. They were either embroidered or printed in tin and carried symbols of rank on the inside. They also wore rank insignia on coat and overcoat collars.

2. Non-commissioned Officers (NCOs)
The non-commissioned officers wore large yellow chevrons on both the combat jacket and overcoat sleeves, indicating their respective ranks and special-isations.

3. Flags and guidons
Each company had its own identifying guidon. From 1862 to 1885, the colors of the American flag with the stars and stripes were adopted, adding the company's letter (3a). The standard was carried by a Guidon Bearer who was normally a non-commissioned officer. From 1885, a red and white bi-colored guidon was adopted, also showing the company and regiment signs (3b). General Custer had his own personal red and blue guidon with two crossed sabres (3c).

Each cavalry regiment also had its own regimental flag with the Arms of the United States embroidered in silk, including the famous American eagle with its wings outstretched and the Latin phrase E Pluribus Unum. The background was usually blue. However, the 10th Regiment was the exception, as shown in the illustration, as it was yellow (3d). Custer's headquarters flag being very similar.

4 Campaign Caps and Hats.
4.a The cap used was a similar to the so-called kepis of French origin (4a). They were normally only worn in garrison, as they quickly became saturated when it rained and offered no protection to the neck from

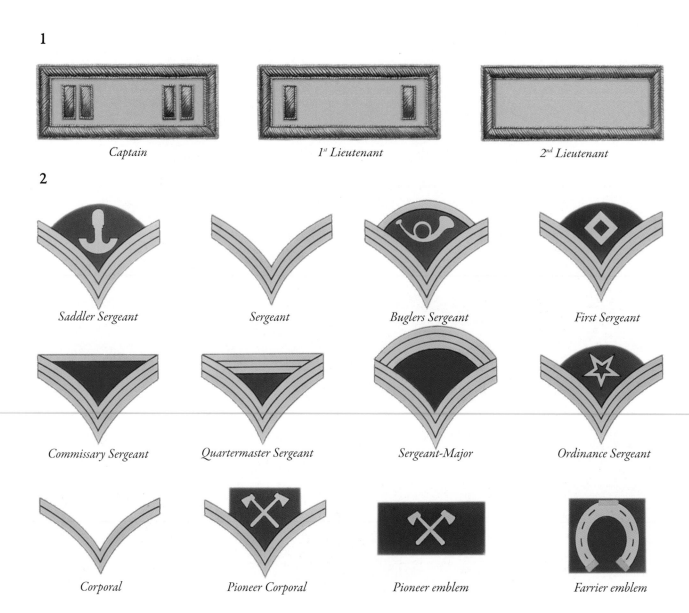

1

Captain *1st Lieutenant* *2nd Lieutenant*

2

Saddler Sergeant *Sergeant* *Buglers Sergeant* *First Sergeant*

Commissary Sergeant *Quartermaster Sergeant* *Sergeant-Major* *Ordinance Sergeant*

Corporal *Pioneer Corporal* *Pioneer emblem* *Farrier emblem* the blazing sun. The models inherited from the Civil War were known by their nickname 'bummer', a later version improved upon this with the 1872 model shown in the illustration.

4.b The first hat emanated from the Civil War and was known as the 'Hardee' or Model 1858 Dress Hat, made of black felt (4b). It had a yellow cord finished with two tassels for the NCOs and troopers. For the officers, this cord was golden and black, or just the latter color, depending on the rank and finished with two decorations in the shape of acorns. Theoretically, it also had one decorative feather for the troops and two for the NCOs. It was in use until 1872, but was normally used without any of the previously mentioned decorations. Later, another hat model was produced, the '1872-pattern folding hat', with wider flaps that could be gathered together at the upper part thanks to a hook fixed to the upper part of the hat, thus completely changing its appear-

ance such that it looked more like the typical French hat chapeau-de-bras. This model was very unpopular and from 1875 others based on the civilian 'East Coast' model with ventilation holes were manufactured. In spite of all the attempts at improving the headdress, civilian hats were always preferred and straw hats were used in hot climates and during warm weather.

4.c The crossed sabres have been the United Stated Cavalry coat of arms since 1851 (4c). In theory, campaign hats and caps usually carried this symbol together with the regiment and company numbers (depending on uniform regulations applied). These symbols were made of tin for the troops and embroidered on a black patch for the officers (the crossed sabres were yellow with the regiment number in silver). It is not uncommon to find contemporary photographs showing hats without any decoration or distinctive marking.

Illustrations by José Ignacio Redondo

CAVALRY WEAPONS

1. Belts

Black leather belt with a steel buckle (1a). This final one remained in use until 1881, when it became authorised for officers only. From the waist hangs the 'cap box' (1b), a small cartridge holder for storing the copper percussion caps for 'cap and ball' type revolvers and that later continued to be used to hold cartridge ammunition. Different models of holster existed for the revolver (1c); the model shown in the illustration was designed for the 'cap and ball' type. In practice, both open or closed, i.e. with closure flap, holsters were employed.

With the introduction of the metal cartridge, various types of belts incorporating cartridge loops to hold the ammunition were adopted (1d). The leather bullet belt was already in existence in 1866, but the troops didn't like it and it was normally replaced with civilian models. In 1876, the production of 30,000 belts with built-in canvas cartridge belts was commissioned. Several models existed, with different production years. The most popular ones were the so-called 'Prairie Belt', 'Christian' and the 'Mills'; the latter is shown in the illustration and already incorporates the new H-shaped buckle used from 1881 (1e).

2. 1860 Model Sabre

It was a slightly curved sabre, based on French models. It had a steel guard and leather grip. The scabbard was also made of steel. High-ranking officers were entitled to carry different models.

3. Knives

They were more of an all-purpose utensil rather than a weapon, very useful for unblocking weapons. The legendary 'Bowie knife' was made in the U.K. and was acquired by soldiers using their own funds (3a). The first Army Issue one was the 1880 campaign model knife (3b).

4. Indian Production

It was not unusual for soldiers to use weapons made or decorated by the Indians. Here, a knife sheath (4a) and holster (4b) are shown.

5. 1851 Model Percussion Navy Colt

This was a .36 calibre 'cap and ball' type revolver. This weapon, and its brother the Colt Army, had the upper part of the frame open. While this made the weapon less robust and accurate, it reduced the accumulation of percussion cap and gunpowder residue making the revolving cylinder mechanism less prone to blockage.

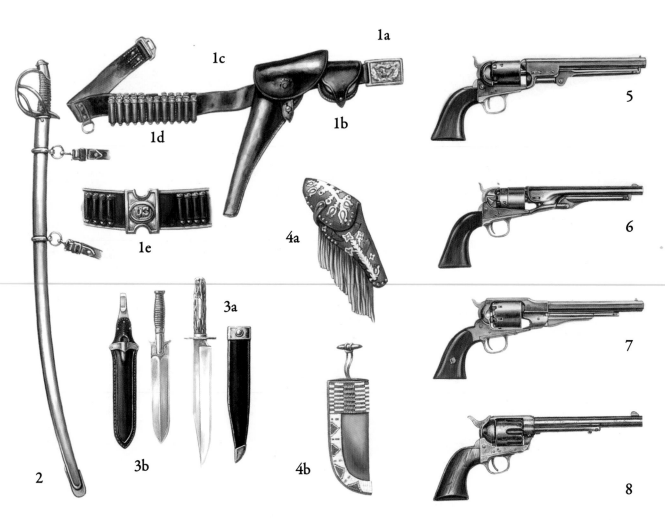

6. 1860 Model Percussion Army Colt

This was a 'cap and ball' revolver frequently used after the Civil War. It was .44 calibre, which gave it greater stopping power and was preferred by the cavalry over the Navy model. A version modified for use with jacketed cartridges appeared later.

7. 1858 Model Percussion Remington

.44 calibre 'cap and ball' type revolver with a more rugged frame than the previous models.

8. 1873 Model Single-Action Army Colt

Its 7 inch barrel and .45 calibre 'central fire' type cartridge provided it with a high level of efficiency and stopping power. Its solid frame design and walnut grips made it robust and reliable.

9. Sharp Carbine

.52 calibre carbine with a linen or paper capsule. Its main virtue was the safety of the firing mechanism, which stemmed from its simplicity.

10.1865 Model Spencer Carbine

It was a .52 calibre repeating carbine. It used metal cartridges that were introduced seven at a time into a tube with a loading spring through the butt (10a). It had a special cartridge holder, called the 'Blakeslee', which contained ten tubes of seven bullets (10b). To store metal cartridges, another types of cartridge holder were modified, such as this one originally designed for the infantry and adapted to carry .50 calibre cartridges (10c).

11. 1873 Model U.S. Springfield Carbine

This was a 45/70 calibre breech-loading Allin breech-block carbine popularly known as the 'Trapdoor'. It had a barrel measuring 22 inches and was the cavalry's basic weapon from its introduction until 1890.

12. Carbine sling

Used for all types of carbines

13. Gatling gun

This was a 45/70 calibre machine gun adopted by the U.S. Army in 1866. Its firing mechanism was based on a multi-tube cylinder (the number of barrels varied according to the model) triggered by a crank. It could fire up to 200 shots per minute. Although it was taken on some campaigns during the Indian Wars, it was neither useful nor popular among the men who hated having to drag these slow contraptions.

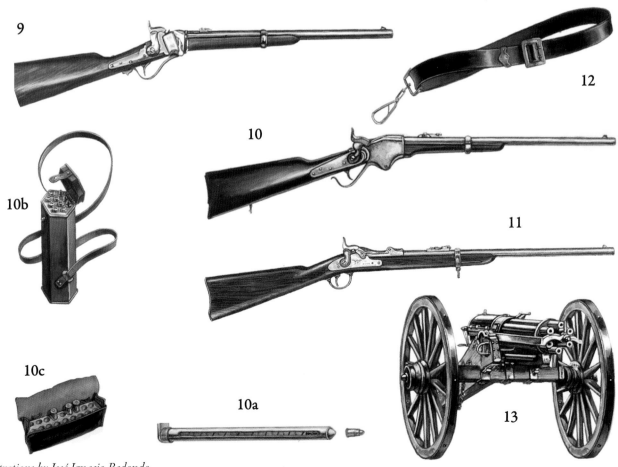

Illustrations by José Ignacio Redondo

THE CAVALRY REGIMENTS

The basic cavalry unit in 1865 remained the regiment that, in theory, was commanded by a colonel. However, command was often designated to the General Staff with operational command being assigned to the lieutenant colonel. According to the 1861 regulation, a regiment comprised 12 companies that tended to be grouped into four battalions of two or three companies each, normally commanded by a major. Each company could be divided into two squadrons, led by a lieutenant. In practice, smaller groups within the squadron could be delimited, commanded by NCOs and these subdivisions were occasionally called squads as in the infantry unit style.

The Company

The widespread dispersion of the regiments in companies along the frontier meant that the basic administrative and operational unit were the companies themselves. Each one was commanded by a captain identified by a letter from 'A' to 'M'. This denomination defined 13 companies within the same regiment; but the letter 'J' was not used, to avoid confusion with the letter 'I' (due to the similar way in which they are written) and with the letter 'A' (because of the similar pronuncia-

tion in English). The twelve remaining letters were left for 12 theoretical companies, according to the 1861 regulation.

The Soldiers Force

The numerical strength of the cavalry regiments and companies varied substantially throughout the Indian Wars. In 1865, the theoretical effective regimental strength was 997 soldiers and officers and 96 for each company. By 1869, government cutbacks had already officially reduced these numbers, setting them at 60 men for a company and limiting the number of its NCOs. It was only after the disaster at Little Big Horn in 1876 that the effective strength was again increased, reaching a maximum of 100 men per company.

However, the cavalry's problems did not only originate from the Washington cutbacks. Desertion and illness was commonplace and it was not unusual for a unit to rely on just half its theoretical affective strength. This weakness affected both the troops and the officers, the latter even more so, as many of them were seconded to the Regimental General Staff or even the Army General Staff in the case of larger units.

REGIMENT COMMAND STRUCTURE

Field Officers: Regiment or Battalion Leaders.
1   Colonel
1   Lieutenant-Colonel
3   Major

Staff Officers: Officers in charge of logistic and administrative tasks and other regimental level specializations.
1   Adjutant Officer (generally a lieutenant responsible for administration)
2   Quartermaster and Commissary Officers
1-2   Surgeon Officers
2   Chief Buglers

Non-commissioned Officers (N.C.O.) and Enlisted Men
1   Sergeant-Major
1   Quartermaster-Sergeant
1   Commissary-Sergeant
1   Saddler Sergeant
1   Veterinary Sergeant
1   Chief-trumpeter
1   Farrier
2   Regimental Hospital Steward
16   Musicians

COMPANY COMMAND STRUCTURE

Line Officers: company or squadron leaders
1   Captain (A)
1   1st Lieutenant (B)
1   2nd Lieutenant (C)

Non-commissioned Officers and Enlisted Men
1   First Sergeant (D)
1   Quartermaster-Sergeant (E)
1   Commissary Sergeant (F)
1   Saddler Sergeant (G)
5   Sergeants (H)
8   Corporals (I)
2   Musicians (generally buglers) (J)
2   Wagoners
2   Farriers (1 of them: K)
78   Privates

HORSE FURNITURE

During the peak of the war against the Indians in 1876, many of the cavalry regiments' horses were still equipped with saddles and other furniture from the Civil War. This equipment was of poor quality given its hasty manufacture and cost cutbacks, essential in order to quickly produce thousands of saddles, bridles and other accessories. The badly cut and died leather gave them an old and tarnished look. While some leather items quickly deteriorated under the harsh climatic conditions of the Great Plains others, such as the bridles and stirrups had to be maintained in good working order.

The U.S. Cavalry regulation saddle was the popular model created by a captain of the 1st Cavalry, George McClellan, in 1855 and it was named after him. The design was based on a Prussian model and remained in use until the First World War with a few modifications. Its wooden frame was very strong and was covered in rawhide. All the saddle pieces were made of black-dyed leather, although it is possible to find models in various hues of brown.

The saddle blanket was placed under the saddle and was made from indigo blue wool. It was

75 " long by 67 " wide, but was folded several times until six layers were obtained. It was trimmed with a 3 " orange stripe.

The saddle was also used to support the rest of the riding equipment. It was most important to avoid overloading the horse. However, on many occasions, especially when campaigns lasted for months and greater quantities of rations, ammunition and forage had to be carried, as well as extra blankets and ponchos, this was unavoidable. On reconnaissance or patrol missions or when pursuing the

Plates A & B

1) 1874 McClellan model saddle
2) Two black leather saddlebags hung from each side of the saddle for storing ammunition, rations, etc.
3) Blanket roll
4) Forage bags carrying horse feed, generally oats.
5) Bag/pouch
6) Nose bag, which was hung from the horse's head for feeding, made of leather and canvas
7) Carbine socket
8) Saddle skirts. They were uncomfortable and the rider often discarded them:
9) Bridles
10) Stirrups. Generally made from walnut or American oak wood, made from a single piece for the troops; the officers' stirrups were made of metal. Some troopers and officers fitted a protective cover at the front.
11) Canteen
12) Tin mug
13) Lariat and picket pin

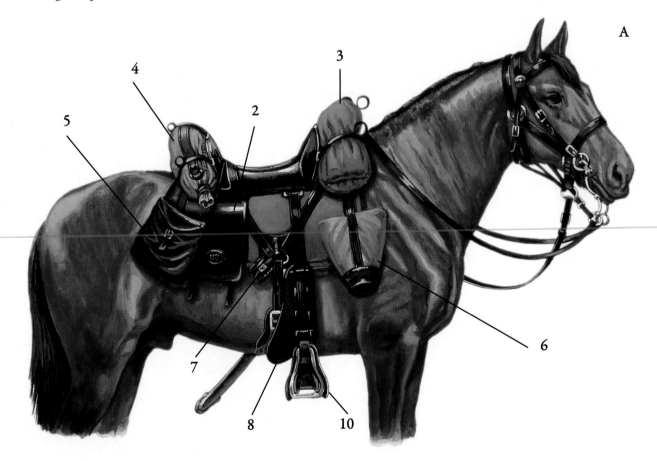

enemy, every unnecessary item was placed in the baggage train. The use of non-regulation articles was also quite common. The officers usually carried different elements including girths made from other materials or a dark blue saddlecloth with a yellow stripe.

C

1
2
3
4
5
6
7

Plate C

1) Binoculars, field glasses and their case.
2) Horse riding gauntlets: They were generally white (White Berlin) or buff.
3) Spurs. They were usually of steel with a simpler design than the officer's gilt/brass ones shown here.
4) 1874 Model canvas and buffalo hide boots, for use in cold temperatures.
5) Riding boots, 1872 Model. They were designed without a distinction between left and right feet. Several models were manufactured with slight variations in design and quality, depending on the supplier.
6) Lariat and picket pin. As trees were rare on the prairies, the only means of picketing a horse was to use an iron stake in the ground.
7) Canteen. Made from metal and covered in canvas or woollen material; some models were stencilled with 'U.S.' on the cover along with the owner's name or other identifying mark.

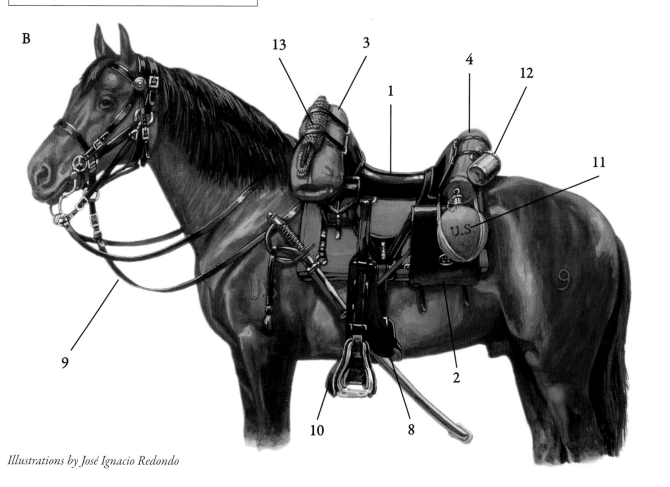

B

Illustrations by José Ignacio Redondo

'Sioux Chief'. By Frederic Remington.

The Indians

"To me, Indian life, with its attendant ceremonies, mysteries, and forms, is a book of unceasing interest. Grant that some of its pages are frightful, and, if possible, to be avoided, yet the attraction is none the weaker. Study him, fight him, civilize him if you can, he remains still the object of your curiosity, a type of man peculiar and undefined, subjecting himself to no known law of civilization, contending determinedly against all efforts to win him from his chosen mode of life." [73]

Through years of John Wayne Movies and earlier Western Dime Novels, the American Indian has been portrayed as a bloodthirsty savage and hater of the paleface. Many of our misconceptions sprang from legends and myths fueled by Hollywood. The celluloid Indian was a blood thirsty savage bent on lifting your scalp.

And in a few cases an enemy's scalp would actually be removed before or after death. Although this practice has been attributed to the Indian's barbaric nature, the true act of scalping was introduced to the American Indian by his sophisticated European counters, the French and the English and dates back to the Middle East in Biblical times.

Stalking and surrounding covered wagons intent on ambush, the Indian has become stereotyped as the classic antagonist and villain. But the true American Indian was peaceful by nature and tied closely to the ecology of the earth. The Redman's utilization of the resources available to him, through animal skins used for his homes and clothing, set him apart as a naturalist and an early day environmentalist. Everything that the Indian needed in life was used to the point that nothing was wasted. Native Americans practiced thriftiness by passing down simple tools, such as hand scrappers made from an animal bone or sharpened stone, to future generations. Because of his great respect for the earth and his fellow man the American Indian was indeed one of the most misunderstood civilizations wrought by the mere fact that the white man did not understand his spiritualism or warrior ways.

More than 14,000 years ago the early American Natives are believed to have come to this continent from Asia via the Bering Straits. Some theories suggest, they came in pursuit of game.[74] Each tribal division settled in a place they came to adapt to. *"While the Whiteman sought to dominate and change the natural setting, the Indian subordinated himself to it."* [169] That same great expanse that extends from the Canadian Rockies to the Gulf of Mexico and from the Mississippi across the Salt Flats to the Pacific Shores was at one time all Indian Country. Over 2.5 Million square miles of wild uncharted prairie inhabited by 270,000 Indians of 125 distinct tribes, some friendly and some hostile to those settlers who would eventually venture onto what we call the Great Plains. Indians were known to be casual and impermanent occupiers of that soil with no notion of ownership, no instrumentalities for recording or transferring title; they roamed over the land as do beasts of the forest, and constructed no permanent settlements.

Early colonists to America saw the Redmen as pagans, almost animalistic in manner, they failed to see their deeply religious and artistic nature and their love of beauty. All of these attributes he expressed in his everyday life.

Dog Dance. Hidatsa Warrior.

TRIBES OF THE INDIAN NATION

1. The North-West
Abenaki, Algonquin, Cayuga, Delaware, Eastern Cree, Erie, Huron, Iroquois, Illinois, Kickapoo, Mohican, Menomini, Miami, Micmac, Mohawk, Narragansett, Ojibwa, Oneida, Onondaga, Ottowa, Penobscot, Pequot, Potawatomi, Sauk-Fox, Seneca, Susquehannock, Tuscarora, Winnebago, Wyandot.

2. The South-East
Apalachee, Biloxi, Caddo, Catawba, Cherokee, Chickasaw, Choctaw, Creek, Muskogean, Natchez, Pamunkey, Powhatan, Seminole, Shawnee, Tuscarora.

3. The Great Plains
Arapaho, Arikara, Assiniboine, Blackfoot, Caddo, Cayuse, Cheyenne, Comanche, Cree, Crow, Dakota (Sioux), Gros Ventre, Hidatsa, Iowa, Kiowa, Mandan, Missouri, Omaha, Osage, Oto, Paiute, Pawnee, Ponca, Sarsi, Shoshone, Ute, Wichita.

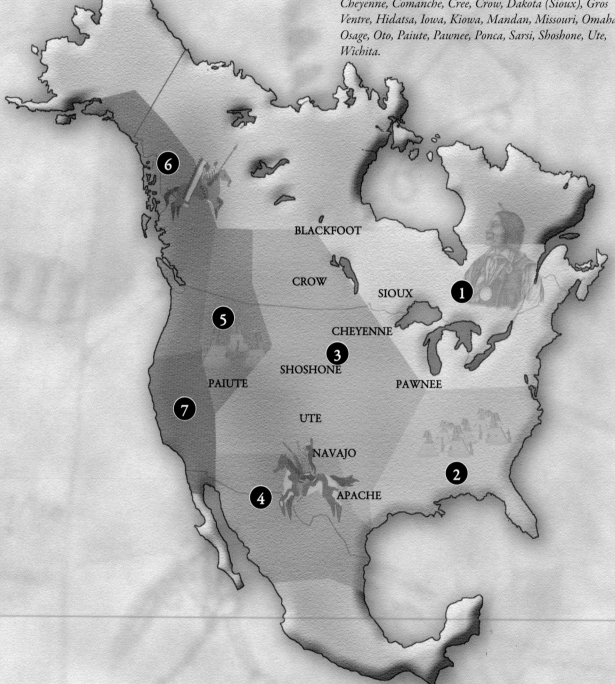

4. The South-West
Acoma Pueblo, Apache, Havasupai, Hopi, Jemez, Laguna Pueblo, Maricopa, Mohave, Papago, Pima, Pueblo, Taos Pueblo, Tarahumara, Tonto, Walapai, Yaqui, Yuma, Zuni.

5. The Colombian Plateau
Coeur d'Alene, Flathead, Kalispel, Kutenai, Nez Perce, Palouse, Spokan, Tenino, Umatilla, Wallawalla, Yakima.

6. The North-West Coast
Bella Coola, Chimakuan, Chinook, Duwamish, Haida, Kusan, Kwakiutl, Nisqually, Nootka, Puyallup, Salish, Shahaptian, Snohomish, Songish, Squamish, Tillamook, Tlingit, Tsimshian, Twana, Yoncalla.

7. California
Chumash, Hupa, Karok, Kato, Klamath, Maidu, Miwok, Modoc, Mono, Pomo, Shasta, Wappo, Washo, Yokut, Yurok.

The Indian had strong family ties and deep commitment to the tribe. These values sustained them as they were pushed westward as the white race practiced their Manifest Destiny. Even with these values, their ties to the land ran deeper. Geronimo said of the Apaches *"when they are taken from these homes they sicken and die."*

Such was the case of tens of thousands of Choctaw, Chickasaw, Creek, Cherokee and Seminole who were forcibly moved from their permanent homes over eight hundred miles to Indian Territory in what would later become known as The Trail of Tears. Over 24,000 Creeks diminished in number to 13,537 after being forced to move to Oklahoma.[75]

"He is neither a luxury nor necessary of life. He can hunt , roam, and camp when and where so ever he pleases, provided always that in so doing he does not run contrary to the requirements of civilization in its advancing tread. When the soil which he has claimed and hunted over for so long a time is demanded by this to him insatiable monster, there is no appeal; he must yield, or, like the car of a juggernaut, it will roll mercilessly over him, destroying as it advances. Destiny seems to have so willed it, and the world looks on and nods its approval."[76]

Although in 1803 President Jefferson authorized the Corps of Discovery to map out and explore the West, the Americans had been perfectly willing to leave it to the Indian and the Buffalo, and as late as 1832 it was viewed as permanent Indian territory where the American Aborigines could pursue their ancestral way of life without interference. During the 1840s the tribes became familiar with the white man, chiefly the French who adopted the Indian ways. As traders and trappers, they integrated into the lifestyle of the various tribes, often times marrying Indian women and having children. In May of 1841 the first immigrant wagon train passed westward along the Oregon Trail known to the Indian as "The Great Medicine Road." With them came the Missionaries who wanted to save their heathen souls, while the English tried to civilize them. Years earlier Pocahontas, daughter of Powhatan, had traveled to England. She shed her leathers for fine lace and took tea in the court of King James.[77] Samoset and Squanto, cultivated a friendship with the Pilgrims and *"directed them how to set their corne, where to take fish and procure other commodities..."* Those experiences conjure images of our traditional Thanksgiving. But yet, through the better part of Indian-White relations a familiar scenario seems to run, *"First the Indians would share their food with the newcomers. Then the supply ships would be delayed and the settlers, having made no attempt to grow a crop, would become demanding. The Indians, with their stores depleted, would refuse aid. Then would come bad feeling, even open hostility."* This proved to be the true clash of values for which Europeans, framed by traditions, failed

'Mandan Village'. By George Catlin.

to grasp in their study of the complexities of the Indian beliefs.[78] For the Indian, his *"integrity of spirit was deeper than conscious reasoning;"* his love of homeland and founded fears of the Whiteman's encroachment, which the Indian likened to *"the horror of dismemberment."* Civilization brought small pox and almost as infamous "Fire Water" which today is as threatening to the Redman as it was a century ago."*He is in danger of becoming a drunkard before he has learned to restrain his appetites, and of being tricked out of his property before he is able to appreciate its value."* [95] Indian resentment increased, *"As the white frontier advanced tribe after tribe fell before new diseases to which they had developed no resistance."* The outbreak of Asiatic cholera, introduced to North America from Europe in 1832 spread like wild fire across the plains.[79]

Angie Debo's "A History of the Indians of the United States" opens with a provocative quote by a Creek Indian Chitto Harjo, *"They (The White men) wanted my country and I was in trouble defending it."* [169] Lakota Mystical Warrior Crazy Horse once stated, *"One does not sell the earth upon which the people walk."* [80] And Tecumseh, a military strategist, who united his people and when asked to sell his lands replied, *"Why not sell the air, the clouds and the great sea...?"*

Although some villages never moved, the Mandan of Dakota lived for generations at the same location, whereas the Plains tribes were in constant migration. Later on with the re-introduction of the horse by Spaniards, they were able to embrace a new hunting culture, dominate a larger portion of warfare on the Plains and became more mobile. *"Indians mounted their ponies, first having fixed their toilets in war paint, and adorned their head and hair with feathers. Also the mane and tail of their ponies, and those having white ponies (which are very plenty amongst them) they daub red paint on so as to look as though they had been wounded."* [81] Horses were a measure of wealth and prowess. Warriors gained honors for the theft and capture of enemy horses. The Comanche, thought by many to be the greatest horsemen in the world, were often described as centaurs; horse and rider appearing as one.[82] Streaking wildly bareback across the western plains, they drop their bodies on either side of their ponies' back, screening themselves from their enemies' weapons and cut loose with arrow or firearm at a full gallop.[83]

"They shall hold the bow and the lance: they are cruel, and will not shew mercy: their voice shall roar like the sea, and they shall ride upon horses, every one put in array, like a man to the battle, against thee..." [84] For the military they had the thankless job of policing

'A Peril of the Plains'. By Frederic Remington.

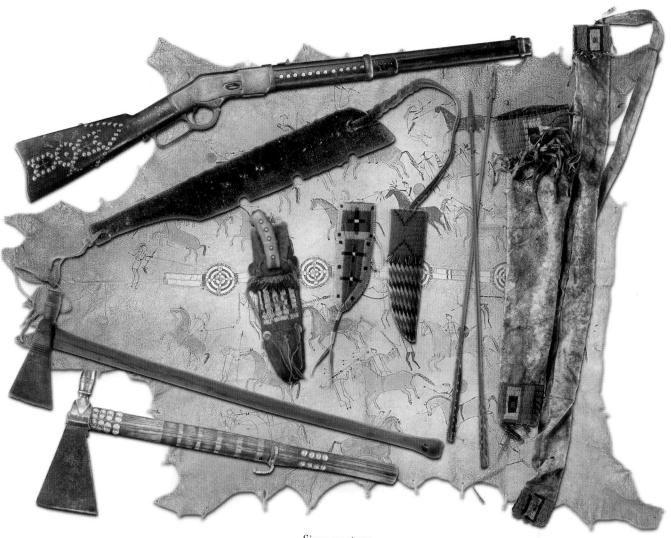

Sioux weapons.

the territories with a total troop force of 27,000 soldiers. And the unlikely task of surrounding ten Indians with one soldier while enforcing policies set in Washington and changing when those policies became obsolete.

Initiation to the west was to learn quickly and adapt skills and knowledge in dealing with a society so diametrically opposite to modern European tactics. Their courage is unquestioned, equaled only by their cruelty.[85] *"...we witnessed one of the finest and most imposing military displays, prepared according to the Indian art of war, which it has ever been my lot to behold. It was nothing more or less than an Indian line of battle drawn directly across our line of march; as if to say: thus far and no farther. Most of the Indians were mounted; all were bedecked in their bright colors, their heads crowned with the brilliant war bonnet, their lances bearing the crimson pennant, bows strung, and quivers full of barbed arrows. In addition to these weapons, which with the hunting-knife and tomahawk are considered as forming the armament of the warrior, each one was supplied with either a breech-loading rifle or revolver, sometimes with both-the latter obtained through the wise foresight and strong love of fair play which prevails in the Indian Department..."*[73]

Although much in want of firearms, the Indian preferred the 3 and a half-foot or 4 foot bow. The Sioux and Crow were known to make the best bows. The arrowheads, fashioned from metal barrel hoops and fastened to the shaft of the arrow by sinew. Arrow wounds were especially dangerous to humans because body fluids would effuse around the point of penetration, which then softened the tendon wrapping holding the head. Thus when the shaft was pulled from the body, the loosened head would remain. If the head was not removed by surgery, such wounds were always mortal.[86]

The Warrior is esteemed above all others who can throw the greatest number of arrows in the sky before the first one falls to the ground. Two Lance a Brule could shoot an arrow clear through a running buffalo as evidenced when he hunted with the Grand Duke Alexis at Red Willow Creek in Nebraska during the winter of '72.

Some tribes though peaceful by nature, never considered peace, but immediately attacked the Spanish or other tribes they deemed trespassing on their hunting grounds. Since the Spanish came to conquer, *"leaving a trail of destruction and death and carrying away captives and slaves."* This justified their extermination of the Indian.

'Visit to Another Tribe'. By Edgar Samuel Paxon.

'Thus Far and No Farther'. By Rick Reeves.

Indian history, however, is more than history of Indian-White relations and dislocations resulting from that relationship. To some the redman has been shamefully treated and betrayed by the white man. Those holding this extreme view are ones who have never lived on the Frontier, for the most part far removed from the Indian, and have not had opportunities of studying the redman in his natural habitat and character. While those in closer proximity think that the Indian has been absurdly pampered by our Government. Incarcerated and confined to areas known as reservations, Indian people endured long years of abuse and prejudice.

"If I were an Indian, I often think that I would greatly prefer to cast my lot among those of my people who adhered to the free open plains, rather than submit to the confined limits of a reservation, there to be the recipient of those blessed benefits of civilization, with its vices thrown in without stint or measure."[73]

At Fort Sill Oklahoma Geronimo spent his final days, known as the "Last Renegade;" he sold small bows, his autograph and buttons off his shirt which he promptly replaced in time for the next unsuspecting white eyed tourist who would squander their money on a piece of authentic Indian history.[87]

At their peak they numbered 8,000 individuals distributed between the Chiricahua, Mescalero, and Tonto Apache tribes. Unlike their plains cousins they chose often to fight on foot rather than horseback. Their reputation for cruelty was matched only by their great endurance, evasion and ability to ambush.[88]

Yet some said of the Apache that, *"They are a gentle people, not cruel, faithful in their friendship, and skilled in the use of signs."* Although they shared a common way of life, they belonged to a dozen or more different tribes speaking languages of a half-dozen totally unrelated groups. So it was for them to communicate through the use of sign language which became the universal talk of the plain tribes.[89] Through smoke signals, mirrors, drums or the water telegraph they have communicated through the ages. Basic paints, colored beads, and use of items from Mother Earth have told stories, gave warnings or guided those who would seek a trail. To the Indian all things were interconnected. All objects had life. And life continued, when this one we know ended, in the Happy Hunting Ground.

Wakan Tanka the Everywhere Spirit was with you and all around you. Your medicine was either good or your judgment was tainted by your impureness of heart.

Nomadic by nature and driven by the pursuit of food sources, the Indian has adapted to the land and it is from the land he finds his means. As the prairies grow lush grasses so do the Indians pursue their main source of food-the Bison. Reliant on the Buffalo for subsistence the warriors could successfully hunt and kill 12 buffalo thus supplying a band of a hundred 12,000 lbs of meat. A similar requirement would be of 120 deer to feed the same band for a month. Before the coming of the whiteman the buffalo numbered some 600 million, thundering across the grasslands and wooded forests of the mid-west.

Although buffalo commonly traveled in small bands of 5 to 50 head, it was not uncommon for a herd to hold up a train for several days while it passed one particular spot. Estimates ranging up to 60 million bison had been calculated in the 1860's with 100,000 hides processed each year since the 1840's. Buffalo hides were being shipped eastward to tanneries that accepted them as alternative sources of commercial leather. Buffalo tongues considered a delicacy by Indian and Non-Indian alike were pickled and canned while whole carcasses rotted on the Plains.

The .50 calibre Sharps alone had a devastating effect on the herds. A single hunter armed with a Sharps Rifle might bag 150 bison per day keeping 15 skinners busy full time. Hides selling from $2.75 would go on to hit an all time high of $5.00. Once the Overland route was established, the Indian felt the whiteman was driving away the buffalo.[79] By 1867 the westward progress of the Union Pacific railroad had driven a wedge through the great bison

L. PATTEN

herds. Indian's superstitious beliefs were that once the buffalo scented the whiteman the bison would not return to that part of the prairie. So destroying the Bison became the overall strategy for subjugating the tribes.

"Destroying the Indian's commissary," commented General Sheridan, *"for the sake of lasting peace, let them kill, skin and sell until they have exterminated the buffalo. Then your prairies will be covered with speckled cattle and the festive cowboy."*

Besides the hides used in the clothing and homes, the Indian utilizes the skin from the buffalo neck to make his war shields. The skin is soaked and hardened with the glue extracted from boiling the bison hooves and when finished allows a surface impenetrable by arrow and curved sufficiently to deflect the path of a bullet.[86]

Theirs' is a system based on courage, yet plagued by duplicity and falsehood. Although we might appreciate their wit and humor and admire their color and pageantry, their passionate fondness of dancing; we must also recognize their brutal side. Young boys of the tribe are raised with warrior ethics in a warrior society. Raiding for them is not only a right, but also necessary training to build self-esteem. A Blackfoot song expressed a common Plains sentiment, *"It is bad to live to be old, better to die young fighting bravely in battle."* [82] Indian culture is based upon permanent war with their neighbors as evidenced by the Chippewa who were successful in driving the Sioux their word for "enemy" from Michigan, Wisconsin and part of Minnesota.[85] In 1851,the Uncpapa stubbornly refused to make peace with the Crow.

Primary to a raid is to steal horses and mules. If homes are burned, settlers killed and scalped; women and children taken captive, then the raid is considered a success. In 1862 the eastern or Santee Sioux under Little Crow perpetrated the Minnesota Massacres.[79] *"Since 1862 at least 800 men, women, and children have been murdered within the limits of my present command, in the most fiendish manner; the men usually scalped and mutilated, their private parts cut off and placed in their mouth; women ravished sometimes fifty and sixty times in succession, then killed and scalped, sticks stuck in their persons, before and after death."*

Sioux tribes who once had formerly lived and hunted on the Platte until gold was discovered in Colorado, now turned to the elders of the Nations. Resistance to this insurgence took a variety of forms- at first alliances, then movements seeking solutions based on native experiences and ideologies. Oglala councilors, composed of older and respected community leaders, sometimes called "the Big Bellies"

Original Oil Painting by L. Patten.
Courtesy of Rowland Chenez.

'The Pony War-Dance'. By Frederic Remington.

adopted various strategies in response to the challenge of incessant encroachment on their lands; treaty diplomacy, or merely leading their bands away from American settlements. These men who sat in councils were basically legislators sometimes called chiefs who evidentially called for outright warfare.

From 1857 until 1882 a state of war existed between the Sioux tribes and the White men encroaching on the plains. In November of 1864 Colonel John Chivington and his Colorado Volunteers deliberately stirred up the Cheyenne hostility resulting in the Sand Creek or Chivington Massacre. Many warriors in the village had been on the war path and fresh scalps of white women and children were found by troops in the village.[79] For those carried off it is certain torture at the hands of these unmerciful savages. If spared, they are usually in for a long hideous night of misery.[85] When a white woman fell into Indian hands she could expect to be forced into the brutal lust of her captor. Indians tend to gamble almost day and night. An Indian smokes incessantly while he gambles. He will gamble all that he owns including his wife. More often than not it is a captured woman from another tribe or a captive white woman who upon tiring of her will gamble or barter her away to another Indian for two horses or such then traded to another before being traded on once again. Should she try to escape her bare feet would be placed into a campfire until every portion of the cuticle was burned away preventing her from running away.[90]

Cheyenne war shield captured at the Battle of Washita owned by General Custer.

Therefore the Military's task is to secure the release of these captives as soon as possible, and hopefully return them home unharmed.

George Custer issued a standing order that should the column come under attack and fear of his wife falling into the Indians hands should occur, the escort was directed to put a bullet in her brain. The old frontiersman adage had always been, *"Keep the Last Bullet for Yourself."*

The ambush is their favorite tactic, and is used both offensively and for defense. War parties rely on swift attacks. First, there is little time available during a raid to engage in a shot for shot contest. The purpose of a raid is to strike fast and leave. Second, the loss of a single warrior takes a lifetime to replace. Indians during a raid on a settlement are cold, cruel and heinous. Their best weapon is fear and terror. The brutal and hideous mutilations of their victims create an unsightly horror dismembered beyond recognition. Once human, they can could only be discerned by the smallest bit of flesh still clinging to clothing of the unfortunate soul.

When warriors rode off to war, they usually dressed in their finest clothes and painted themselves not to frighten their enemy, but to impress the Everywhere Spirit should they be killed. The purpose of the paint was to prepare for their burial and to radiate a handsome and respectable appearance in the afterlife. *"Indians are very fond of bright and gaudy colors, and if they see any trinket which they like they will have it regardless of cost, if they have the price*

Chief Gall.

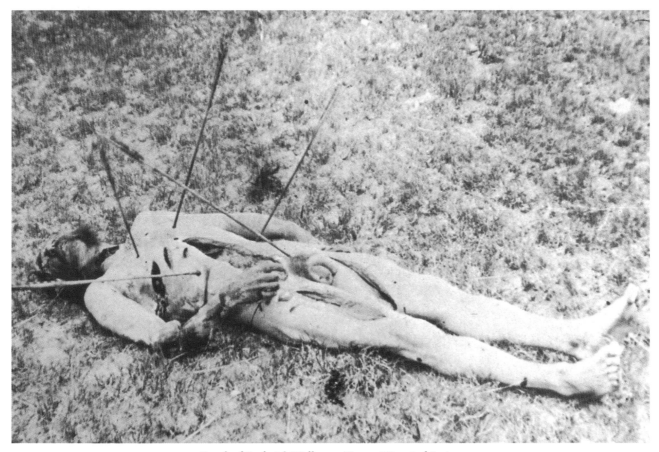

Death of Frederick Wyllyams. Kansas Historical Society.

Sitting Bull.

of it in their possession. And jewelry they all wear. Of course, it's nothing but brass or German silver. Some of them will have a cord around their necks filled with all kinds of stuff just so it shines. I have seen some with rings on all their fingers-not only one on a finger, but 3 or 4 on each. And for earrings, it's awful. They will be from 2 to 2 1/2 inches across and from 3 to 4 in each ear, one above the other. And the holes in the outer edge of their ears are as large as an eyelet in a shoe." [81]

Streaming in the wind were their large headdresses sometimes referred to as War Bonnets, made from buckskin turbans or the crowns of traded or captured slouch hats affixed with eagle, hawk or turkey feathers, often earned or given in allegiance from other warriors in the tribe. Sometimes the standing feathers would encircle the crown and flow at length to a long train that reached in some cases to the ground. They were never without their Hudson Bay trade blanket even in warm weather when they draped it over their arm or wore it like a cloak. Their legs were covered by their long breach cloths and leggings often fashioned from trade blankets or animal skins with beads and fringe at the seams. Their feet were covered by soft tanned buckskin moccasins with intricate bead work or quills in various shades or colors, the soles being made of tough durable buffalo leather. By the 1800's the traditional buckskin shirt was being replaced by trader's cloth and cotton fabric shirts manufactured by the whiteman. Warrior Societies continued the tradition of the "War Shirt" made from hides and decorated with beads, scalps and feathers all honors earned in combat.

Each tribe was composed of many warrior societies. Dog Soldiers, ages 17-37 were represented by at least one family member. Hotamitaneo or Dog Soldiers generally lead in battle and of the Cheyenne they are the most dreaded. Woksikitaneo or Fox Men usually proceed Himoiyogis or Those With Headed Lances, followed by the Mahohivas Red Shield Owners and the Himatanohis, Those with the Bow String. The last were the Hotaminasow or Foolish Dogs mostly made up of younger warriors not yet proven in battle. They make up part of the ten clans of the Cheyenne

Oglala - James Lone Elk.

Crow War Shirt.

including the Heviquesnipahis, Hevhaitaneo, Masikota, Omisis, Sutaio, Wotapio, Oivimana, Hisiometaneo, Oqutogona and Hownowa. They were headed by forty four chiefs who when it came time for council would send out forty four painted sticks to all the villages.[91] Entrance into such societies was accomplished by obtaining coups against an enemy. Evidence was sometimes exhibited by weapons wrenched from an enemy's hands in battle, possessions, captured women or horses. When groups approached each other, the initial actions consisted of attempts to frighten the other side, and to show bravery. Chanting war songs or "Wolf Songs" they go into battle with the object of insulting the enemy, rather than killing him. Counting coups or touching the enemy brings greater honors than taking of a life. This touch could be performed by either hand or short weapon at close quarters. A coups might be made with a quirt or a special coups stick varying in length but almost always adorned

'The Buffalo Dance'. By Frederic Remington.

Buffalo Bill.

with paint, feathers and scalps of enemies. Sometimes curved at the end it was similar to looking like a whiteman's cane, but longer and often displayed in front of the warrior's lodge where all the tribe could know of his achievements in battle. The highest honor fell to the first touch, with three consecutive honors awarded for those who touched the enemy next. Other warriors might rush up to each touch the enemy up to four times. After the fourth touch no more points were accumulated. Many warriors felt that to touch a live enemy or one who had been fallen in combat was equally honorable. Many times the enemy might feign death only to deliver a fatal blow to an opposing warrior attempting to count coups on him. Another example might be to spare the life of an enemy in battle, touching him in a humiliating way that would steal his honor. The act of killing under any circumstance was never rated as credit to a warrior. When an actual death occurred in combat each warrior who had killed some enemy followed such an act with a death wail many times misconstrued as a "Yell of Triumph." When in fact it was a wail of utter sadness at the taking of a human life and prayer for forgiveness to the Everywhere Spirit. Most ceremonies before or after a battle consisted of the death wail for those who may be killed and those who actually were. But since Indians were unwilling to accept even a few casualties, under most circumstances they simply withdrew. The feeling of awe at

taking life was also felt probably to a lesser degree-when animals were killed. To the American Indian everything possessed a living soul. Therefore every part of an animal which when killed was either consumed or utilized for clothing or tools, insuring it had not died in vain. Indians unlike non-Indians, never hunted for sport. The sorrow one might endure at killing of an enemy may last up to 30 days in which time the warrior blackened his face, his hair flowed loose and his general appearance neglected and unkempt. Such was the shame that most battles if one or two participants were killed on either side the whole conflict may be called as both sides retreated from the field.

Most myths recounting the warrior's lust for torture were greatly exaggerated as the act of torture was performed in a symbolic gesture of purification and bravery. Those on the receiving end may have thought differently as *"...they persisted in the hellish work until every inch of the bodies of the unhappy men was haggled, and hacked and sacrificed, and covered with clotted blood."* [92]

When a full-blown battle occurred and half of the opposing forces were killed the victors allowed the defeated to surrender and treated the survivors to a big feast and then released them "on parole" as they owed their lives to the victorious band. The survivors were from that moment on honor bound not to attack or make war upon those who had spared them. If they ever should, they ran the risk of capture and ultimate torture.

If a warrior undergoing torture could display fortitude and bravery defying his tormentors to do their worst and survive, in most cases he was nursed back to recovery, praised by his torturers, released or persuaded to become a permanent member of their tribe. *"...the Indian forfeits his claim to the appellation of the noble redman. We see him as he is, and, so far as all knowledge goes, as he has been, a savage in every sense of the word; not worse, perhaps, than his white brother would be, similarly born and bred, but one whose cruel and ferocious nature far exceeds that of any wild beast of the desert."* [73]

In 1869, President Grant appointed a commission of nine men to examine all matters pertaining to Indian Affairs. Their findings reported *"The history of government connections with the Indians is a shameful record of broken treaties and unfilled promises."* [93]

Custer always believed peace could have lasted longer than the outbreak of '74, had diplomacy and proper treatment of the tribes been practiced over government duplicity. [33]

The period between 1869 to 1873, saw little campaigning on the frontier. Armstrong now had achieved a celebrity status in the west and was sought out by diplomats, industrialists and foreign dignitaries. As the railroads pushed west the frontier became a backyard playground for the rich and famous. Custer's articles for "Turf, Field and Farm" lured curiosity seekers and accomplished hunters to the plains in quest of deer, antelope, elk and bison. In a six month period Armstrong hosted over a hundred excursionists. At the same time pulp novelists were churning out such titles as "Scouts of the Prairies" and "Life on the Border." William F. Cody played a prominent role and was encouraged to reprise his role as "Buffalo Bill" for numerous hunts and exhibitions. [94] The west once a place of mystery and misery suffered by the early pioneers became an experience that could be purchased for admission at the price of a railroad ticket.

Blackfoot warrior.

Lieutenant Colonel George A. Custer and the Grand Duke Alexis, January 1872. By James A, Scholten.

Hunting in the West

When the last of the Cheyenne had come into the reservations subjugation of the South West was complete. And much like when the Civil War had ended Armstrong was restless. The mundane could not sustain him. If he could not live breathlessly on the edge, he was not living. He had approached every moment of his life as a contest, a challenge, from card games to the pursuit of deer or buffalo, always pitting himself against nature.

For some people solitude was golden, they were content to complacently sit and let life come to them or pass before their eyes.

Custer ran toward life at the speed of a Jupiter Locomotive. Seeing a single star or the flicker of flame from a campfire miles across the prairie allured him. He was always looking beyond the next ridge.

Like the Mountain Men who were amongst the first white men to venture west. They came into contact with the people of the Nations, they interacted and learned the ways of the Indian. Learned to hunt and trap, adapt to the land and to assimilate into the west.

First they traded, dressed and married into the tribes and from their knowledge of game and of the trail they became the great scouts of the west. Men like Comstock, Cody and California Joe; these were the men who tutored Custer and made him the Plainsman he was to become. Although his role as a soldier occupied a larger part of his time, Custer entertained a plethora of hunters and western enthusiasts.

Hunting which had its genesis in the pursuit of practical nourishment such as deer, elk or antelope first brought the tribes to this continent, now was pursued as food, recreation and trade. The pelts of fur bearing animals were used to barter for goods the whiteman introduced to the plains. Fashionable

Custer's most famous scouts: William F. Cody (Buffalo Bill), Moses Milner (California Joe) and William Averill Comstock (Medicine Bill), the grand nephew of James Fenimore Cooper. By C. Gómez.

Lieutenant Colonel George A. Custer, by James A, Scholten, January 1872. From an original cabinet-sized insert, published in "Photographic World".

his horses and his weapons of choice. Approached by Matthew Barker, field editor for the popular magazine of the huntsman, "Turf, Field and Farm" Armstrong agreed to supply them with adventures of his hunts in the west. Matthew's brother, Kirkland Barker had been the Civil War Mayor of Detroit, and was known by the sobriquet of "K. C. Barker." Owner of the American Eagle Tobacco Company and purveyor of America's Cup the prestigious and most coveted sailing and yachting trophy, that passed between Britain and the United States over their years of boating competition, Barker was also noted for giving Custer his two favorite Scotch stag hounds, Maida and Blucher. As President of the Audubon Club of Detroit Barker gladly received the numerous gifts sent to him by his fast and famous friend, G. A. Custer. Later when Armstrong learned and developed his skills as a taxidermist he was able to send entire trophies and whole preserved specimens to the Audubon Club to back up his fascinating and prolific accounts in the "Turf, Field and Farm" where he wrote under the name he gave himself, "Nomad." [96]

"I have hunted foxes in Ohio, deer and turkey in Michigan, as well as in Texas, and alligators in the bayous along the Red River, but never until the past season have I enjoyed an opportunity of hunting and killing buffalo. As my later experience has proved more successful and gratifying..." wrote Armstrong. *"A pistol shot fired against the tough hide of a buffalo, will, nine times out of ten, produce no other effect than to infuriate him, and woe unto the luckless horse or hunter who allows himself to be overtaken in one of these mad charges... I have scarcely, if ever, encountered a more dangerous enemy than a wounded and infuriated buffalo bull, who, seeing escape fruitless, determines 'to fight it out on the line.' At such times neither man nor beast seems to possess any terrors for him... If the Spanish bull is more terrible or bold than an enraged buffalo bull, I can say, 'from the crafts and assaults' of all such, 'deliver us'... The buffalo when alarmed, always runs against the wind. I never knew an exception to this rule, neither have I ever heard any reason or cause assigned... the plains are covered with buffalo, and when the latter are so fat as to be unable to run fast, it is an easy matter to ride into a herd and bring down or disable an unlimited number... Gradually a spirit of rivalry sprang up... the party killing the fewest buffalo was to provide a champagne supper for the winning side. To verify the number of*

in Europe, beaver pelts were used in hats and other skins from wildcats, bears, wolves and coyotes were eagerly sought after.

Where once hunting had been a crucial component for the hunting and gathering societies, it now became an industry that out stripped its essential food source and became a competitive pastime for the aristocratic, wealthy and sport hunters seeking trophies as a sign of their hunting prowess.

The American prairies were teeming with mule and white-tailed deer, antelope, moose, elk, bear, bighorn sheep and bison. Equally pursued were all matter of rabbit, red fox, beaver , bobcat, cougar, wolf and coyote. Feathered species of grouse, turkey, bobwhite quail, ducks and Canadian geese were being mounted by taxidermists and displayed in offices, studies and luxury halls of castles and estates in the East and Europe.

And when people spoke of "The West," Custer's name was synonymous with action, adventure and wildlife. His exploits and hunts became a conversation of notoriety. As important as his dogs had become from his hunts in Texas, so had interest in

Engraving showing different stages of the Buffalo hunting.

GATHERING THE TONGUES

Berghaus

Champagne Dinner

COUNTING THE TONGUES

buffalo killed it was required that the tongue of the animal must be produced." [8]

This part of the buffalo proved to be a delicacy and tasted much like prime rib. The camaraderie of the hunts were as much a part of the excursions as was the actual bringing down of the bison. K. C. Barker also, an avid sportsman spent as much time as possible on the Kansas prairie with Armstrong in pursuit of the various four legged and feather bearing quarry. The moment that Indian Hostilities terminated, Custer solicited Barker to come to Kansas to hunt buffalo. The hunt proved a success for the sportsmen but a sad occasion when the General's favorite hound Maida was shot accidentally by one of the hunters. [96]

"With little forethought or prudence several of the hunters opened fire upon the buffalo while the latter was contending with the dogs. Maida had seized hold of the buffalo, and while clinging to its throat was instantly killed by a carbine ball fired by some one of the awkward soldiers who accompanied the party..." [7]

Knowing the Ex-Mayor to be also an admirer of good horse flesh, Custer wrote Barker, from Big Creek near Fort Hays, Kansas, in September of 1869 *"... I had two Englishmen hunting with me the other day, they said Dandy was the finest hunter they had ever seen being so well broken".*

Libbie remembered the hunt to her girlfriend Laura Noble in a letter written September 19, *"buffalo hunting has been the real excitement of the summer. Ladies had been debarred the sport until the cavalry ladies came out this spring but Autie wanted me to go so I did and since then the ladies are expected... When we go on a hunt we usually go out from here about ten miles and establish a temporary camp so that we come in from the hunt at night get dinner and sleep on the ground in tents we take out. As the buffalo are not much nearer than twenty miles, we all start out in the morning and rare pretty sight it is. Perhaps twenty officers and fifty soldiers on horseback, three or four ambulances and two or three wagons. The latter are taken out to bring back the choice parts of the buffalo that are killed. Sometimes we see the buffalo for miles before the chase begins. Not a tree is seen out here except on the streams. The buffalo*

graze until we are almost on them. The horse men prepare for the chase by strapping saddles tighter loading carbines and pistols... and deciding which part of the company heads off and which goes in rear of the herd. It is magnificent sport. Only a capital rider can shoot buffalo. For though the prairie looks so level, it is actually very hard to ride over. The three reporters of the N.Y. Times, Herald and a Columbus paper all came to grief, but such slight affairs we could afford to laugh. One was thrown, another shot and slightly wounded his horse, another was lost for a few hours. The wagons and ambulances and my carriage follow fast after the hunters when the chase begins and we are in at the death of many a noble animal... the general was getting up a grand hunt for the two English noblemen Lords Paget and Waterpark... charming and unassuming and able to rough it. Though awkward looking, they rode well. They killed 13 buffalo. I was of course prepared to dislike them and mentally called them 'snobs' before seeing them but such good breeding and genuine kind heartedness made them many friends. They 'took' to Autie as they are so fond of hunting and horses and dogs. I wish so very much we could accept their repeated and cordial invitation to visit them. . . We have had some other 'highnesses' out here before this party but they were not to compare with the last. Doesn't a hundred and twenty six buffalo killed seem a great many for three days? But we had fine success and the prairie seemed black with monsters when the chase began. You can't dream how quickly the herd will disappear after the chase begins and how very fast the buffalo can run. Autie killed seven in one day without leaving the saddle. Even such good riders as our officers are get an occasional tumble for they go at such a breakneck speed but if they do it scarcely ever hurts them as most of them are hardy healthy stalwart men. But the penalty of a tumble is to pay a basket of champagne and we have had considerable wine to drink this summer, forfeit wine I mean" [22]

When The two English Lords prepared to leave for home, in appreciation for the hunt they presented Armstrong and his brother Tom two Galand and Somerville revolvers. [48]

With little or no Indian uprising in sight on the Frontier, Custer was sent to Elizabethtown, Kentucky for two years of reconstruction duty. Certainly to all concerned a let down from the excitement and adventure of the plains, *"Imagine yourself your grandmother to get an idea of this place."* Wrote Libbie, *"Everything is old, particularly the women... The old standing corner clock has not been*

Kirkland C. Baker.

allowed to run down for forty-five years. The dog is sweet sixteen and can scarcely walk... The most active inhabitant of the place is a pig." [15]

Chasing Moonshiners, Knights of the White Camelia and Ku Klux Klansmen the Seventh settled into the role of a police force in the southern states.

Buffalo hunt, near Big Creek, Kansas. Custer is the first on the left. September 1869. By W. J. Philips.

Custer posing in Omaha in 1872. The seal skin cap was a gift of the Grand Duke.

This assignment was broken only briefly, when the Grand Duke Alexis toured the United States in the winter of '72. It was only five years before that the United States purchased Alaska "Seward's Folly" from Russia for $7.2 Million, a bit less than two cents an acre.[100] Now the twenty-one year old third son of Czar Alexander II had come West to see, "The Frontier before it's Gone."

The Union Pacific's Special Train adorned with American and Russian flags, consisted of five Pullman cars, two sleepers, two parlor coaches and an elaborate hotel dining car. Custer joined the

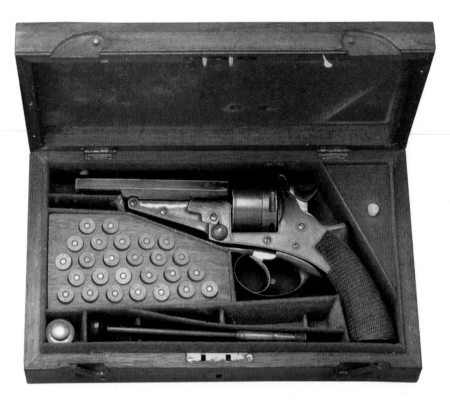

Tom Custer's Galand and Somerville revolver.

entourage in Omaha on January 12 and stayed with the Nobleman for over a month. *"Custer was a constant companion of the Grand Duke for they had taken an instantaneous liking to each other at the first meeting."* [97]

His arrival and view of the country was best documented and described in detail by William W. Tucker who accompanied the Grand Buffalo Hunt to Red Willow Creek just forty miles south of Fort McPherson in Nebraska. Besides a retinue of Russian diplomats and guards, in all the hunting party numbered over 500. Two companies of cavalry and the Second Cavalry band were all under the command of General Innis Palmer.[98] Alexis was pleased to make the acquaintance of William F. Cody "Buffalo Bill" who along with Armstrong scouted for the herds.

The Duke and General Sheridan traveled to the campsite (an eight hour journey)in an army ambulance drawn by four beautiful steeds. Buffalo Bill rode along side of the carriage as well as Custer and numerous officers of cavalry. The Russian Cossacks dressed in their red and green coats and hats were entertaining all as they jumped from their horses to the numerous wagons and conveniently back into their saddles.[100] Frank Thompson who was in charge of the Duke's Train had not been given a horse and was loaned the use of "Buckskin Joe" Cody's mount. Some of the black teamsters kept pointing and exclaiming every time Thompson rode past them. *"Am I not riding this horse alright?"* Thompson inquired of one of the Mule Skinners.

"Yes, sir; you ride all right."

"Then why are they guying me?"

"Why sir, are you not the king?"

"The king? Why did you take me for the king?"

"Because you are riding that horse. Nobody rides that horse but Buffalo Bill. We all supposed you was a king, for that is Buffalo Bill's personal mount Buckskin Joe!" [101]

Spotted Tail and his Brule warriors were enticed with twenty wagon loads of provisions and a thousand pounds of tobacco, to be part of the hunt, entertaining His Royal Highness with Sham Battles and War Dances. They arrived in a flourish when Whistler staged a mock attack on the party. Buffalo Bill and the driver of the ambulance were able to secure a safe haven for the Duke and General Sheridan on an island in Medicine Lake Creek. Meanwhile Custer and some of the Cavalry pursued the Indians in a desperate counter charge where no one was hurt, but many laughs and handshaking took place between the antagonists and their vanquished foes, who'd only a few short summers before had traded live rounds and real arrows.[99] Now animosities were set aside, even Pawnee Killer, no longer espoused to be Armstrong's old nemesis.[1] The Boy General later even accompanied the braves on a Indian Buffalo Hunt performed and executed in the ancient way of the tribes. The site christened "Camp Alexis" was situated on four acres of low grassy level ground which Captain James Egan and the troops of the Second Cavalry had removed snow (in some cases up to 18 inches deep) in order to erect forty of the Army's best wall tents, two large carpeted hospital tents and a series of teepees erected on the opposite bank of the creek.[1]

The hunt began the next morning at 9 AM. It was the Grand Duke's 22nd Birthday and it was promised that he would bring down the first bison.[102]

Outfitted in European hunting attire consisting of jacket and trousers of gray wool trimmed in green bearing buttons of Imperial Russian Coat of Arms, and an Astrakhan Turban, Alexis was armed with a wild boar dagger and Smith and Wesson .44 Russian Revolver. It was with this weapon, one of a quarter million he had contracted the firm to ship to Russia, that he proclaimed he would dispatch his first buffalo.[103]

His first pass at the herd proved undaunted, unloading the Smith and Wesson to no refrain, until Buffalo Bill loaned him Buckskin Joe and his favorite rifle "Lucretia Borgia."

"Now's your time!" Shouted Cody and the Springfield kicked like a mule bringing down one of the largest bulls in the herd. In his ecstasy The Grand Duke threw the rifle to the ground, cracking the stock and let loose a *"a series of howls and gurgles like the death song of all the fog horns and calliopes ever born."*[104]

With his boar's knife he severed the bison's tail and began swinging it above his head as a signal to the Cossacks who immediately came to his relief with baskets of Champagne.

That evening in camp before the bonfires and Chinese lanterns, the Grand Duke recounted his exploits of the day and the Brule warriors performed ceremonial dances and sham fights for the hunters' entertainment. Much taken by Spotted Tail's young daughter both Armstrong and Alexis made polite overtures, Armstrong shamelessly

presenting earrings which he placed in the lovely lobes of the comely maiden.[105]

The next morning found the warriors mounted to perform one more hunt before the Grand Duke, in the ancient manner of "The Horsemen of the Plains." Along beside them rode Armstrong his hair free flowing above his hunting skins not much separating him from these children of the prairie, for "Long Hair" was known to have *the heart of an Indian."*

Two Lance, a young brave of 17 winters shot an arrow through a charging bull and presented the relic to Alexis, who prized it above all gifts bestowed upon his American journey. Before the Nebraska snows melted the Duke had scored eight fine specimens of the Prairie Bison. "Buffalo Bill" was asked to prepare the heads and hides for shipment to Mother Russia while Armstrong continued to entertain and educate the Grand Duke to the ways of the west and the Mysteries of Mammoth Cave. His tour of the Southern States now included the General's wife Libbie as they traveled by steamboat to New Orleans, where the Duke was toasted and honored at Mardi Gras introducing the official theme song that still holds to this day, "If Ever I Cease to Love." Boarding the Russian Ship Svetlana Alexis bid "Do Svidaniya" (good bye) and headed home to his beloved Russia.

Lieutenant Colonel George A. Custer and Grand Duke Alexis, January 1872. By James A, Scholten.

Sitting Bull with his nephew One Bull (1884).

Upon the High Yellowstone

Three years from our Country's Centennial, and the Nation was realizing its place in the Industrial Revolution.

As the West became more populated, the mysteries of the plains were diminished.

The Iron Horse now dominated the scene, and rapid travel brought rapid change. Those treaties made with the five civilized tribes following the Civil War opened vast amounts of land to Public Domain and encouraged the settlement and establishment of towns along Rail Road Right of Way. Some had naively thought that the Buffalo, the Indian and Modernization could co-exist. The increase in white settlers, opportunists and the polarization of the two cultures would eventually erupt in war.

"When the Railroad met the Buffalo, the Iron Age met the Stone Age, the machine arrived in the garden, and the West was changed forever." [106]

Towns grew along the tracks, settlers came west, goods found their way east. Tales of the inhospitable prairie salved by the cosmopolitan growth of the new frontier. What had taken Lewis and Clark two and a half years was reduced to nine days. Minimized to mere hours of travel by train where once the Conestoga rolled for weeks. [107]

With the planting of the Golden Spike, East met West, united the continent, connecting one coast to the other, and was toasted from New York to San Francisco.

Investors clamored for stocks, businesses prospered and the wealthy got richer.

Still the upper plains lay yet unexplored. Surveyors were sent out to map the region despite the repeated warnings from The Hunkpapa Medicine Man Tatanka Iyotanka, Sitting Bull not to enter the Yellowstone Country. That country long seceded to the Lakota was all but dormant. Treaties did not allow for determination and construction of the Railroads. But while violations of those treaties was never a concern before, thinly veiled, corporate interests found the necessary loop holes and the American financier Jay Cooke found the finances for the project to begin. [108]

Engraving showing one of the many indiscriminate killing of buffalo that occurred after the arrival of the railroad.

The Seventh's Regimental Band led by Felix Vinatieri. Dakota Territorial Museum Photograhic Archives.

Like a stick stirred in a bee hive the braves turned their stingers on the surveyors traversing for future tracks of the Northern Pacific Rail Road.

By the Spring of '73, Custer's sojourn in the South was coming to a end. Where he had amused himself purchasing remounts for the Army and adding to his own remuda of thoroughbreds, he'd also won and lost on a race horse jockeyed on his own behalf. "Frogtown" had trumped the best in show but never quite taken the cup the late Don Juan would surely have realized had not a bug brought his brief stud to an end on a farm in Michigan.

Dandy his tried and true was joined by yet another great horse christened Victory, whom he called Vic.

Loading the horses and the Regiment first on River boats and then on trains they soon arrived in Yankton, the seat of the Dakota Territory. Armstrong always particular about every detail, upon arrival reestablished the camp in a new location despite the threatening weather that saw temperatures plummet and the rain changed to snow. It proved to be their bitterly cold introduction to the harsh environment of the Northern Plains. Severe snow fell for over forty eight hours to the chagrin of the soldiers and the towns people who charitably opened home and hearth to save the Seventh.

Prolonged exposure caused the General to fall severely ill and he was only able to weather the storm in the Spartan accommodations of an abandoned cabin on the outskirts of town. Eliza Brown, the general's cook and domestic who had been with him since the war years, had recently left to be married. After long years of dedicated service with the Custers she had been replaced by Mary Adams who now along with Libbie administered to the Buckskin Cavalier during the unforgiving Dakota Blizzard.

Reassessing damage to the command and equipment allowed for several days delay in departure in which the Town of Yankton took advantage hosting a Grand Ball in honor of the Regiment. The composer and musical arranger for the evening was a gifted and talented Italian conductor named Felix Vinatieri who's impression upon Armstrong convinced him to offer the title of "Band Master of the Seventh" stepping in for the ubiquitous John Kaufman who was forced to stay behind in Memphis, Tennessee due to bad health.[109]

Maestro Vinatieri comfortably in the saddle of a white horse preceding the sixteen member band while the actual Colonel of the Regiment, Samuel D. Sturgis who had now joined up with them, was at the head of the Command. The Seventh wheeled into formation and was reviewed by Governor John Burbank and an honor escort of distinguished towns people as the "GarryOwens" departed for the High Yellowstone.

The Steam vessel "Miner" would accompany the command up the Missouri River. General Sturgis transferring to one of the comfortable cabins on board the Coulson Packer all the way to Fort Rice. While Armstrong, with Libbie at the head of the 10 Companies of Cavalry would travel horseback across country paralleling the Missouri.

The fort was established in July of 1864, and had seen extensive activity two summers ago when Major J. N. C. Whistler had departed with the 22nd Infantry to be an escort for the Northern Pacific Surveyors. The two month expedition was confronted by hostiles and detained by heavy snows in the Badlands yet had completed 600 miles, before returning to winter in garrison.[112]

The arrival of the command at Rice found a post situated on the west bank of the Missouri River. *"A*

Fort Rice.

rickety old ferry boat took us across the river when we made a halt near Fort Rice." Wrote Libbie while much to her and Autie's dismay their luggage and all their belongings had sat on the pier where weather had mildewed and destroyed a lot of their personal and cherished items including Libbie's Bridal Gown. *"Strange to say the river was no narrower than it was so many hundreds of miles below where we started. The river was muddy, and full of sand bars. We bravely began to drink the water, when the glass had been filled long enough for sediment to partially settle. We learned after a time to settle the water with alum and finally became accustomed to the taste."* [110]

General David S. Stanley drew the assignment of protecting a railroad survey party against the Sioux once again and began the march with one company of the 6th Infantry, four of the 8th, six companies of the 9th, three companies of the 17th and five companies of the 22nd Infantry; 10 companies of the Seventh Cavalry under the command of Lt. Col. Custer; 250 wagons with enough supplies for two months, 1500 mules, 800 horses, 600 cattle, two Rodman rifled guns. A grand total of about 1,500 officers and enlisted men departed Fort Rice on June 20.[111] Mrs. Custer and Maggie had departed by steam vessel with General Terry to St. Paul three days prior. Mary Adams for the first time in the field accompanied the command cooking for the General and playing nurse maid to brother Tom and a number of officers who now counted themselves part of the Custer Clan. Mary said *"Tell Miss Libbie I like it better out here than I thought I would."*

General David Stanley.

Major George Forsyth, who'd been a mainstay on the staff during the years in Kansas and actively participated in the Grand Buffalo Hunt was replaced by the President's son Second Lieutenant Fred Grant. Of the forty or so civilians and including the surveyors rode the sutler Augustus Baliran and veterinarian Dr. John Honsinger both men shared a kindred interest in nature and prehistoric fossils. All of this rounded out by a contingent of Arikara scouts and three supply steamers.

To Armstrong he was in his element. He was back on the frontier leading his command and pursuing game which was in abundance, *"I never saw such fine hunting as we have had constantly since we left Rice. I have done some of the most remarkable shooting I ever saw and it is admitted to be such by all...[22] The following list exhibits but a portion of game killed by me: Antelope, 41; buffalo, 4; elk, 4; black tail deer, 4; American deer, 3; white wolf, 2; geese, prairie chickens, and other feathered game in large numbers. The number of animals killed is not so remarkable as the distance at which the shots were executed. The average distance at which the forty-one antelope were brought down exceeded 250 yards by actual measurement. I rarely obtained a shot at an antelope under 150 yards, while the range extended from that distance up to 630 yards."* [113]

But his greatest accomplishment was described as "King of the Forest", *"for such was the appellation bestowed upon the magnificent elk of which I write. And with a hunter's pride I will ask you to glance at the long, deep scars on the ears and sides while I recount to you how, after being wounded by my rifle and pursued by my noble stag-hounds, the elk was forced to leap into the river, followed by the dogs... The combat in the water was one of the finest and most exciting hunting scenes I ever witnessed. As I stood on the bank, rifle in hand, and within twenty paces of the quarry, I trembled for the lives of my brave dogs. The water was such depth as enabled the elk to stand on terra firma while the dogs were compelled to swim...[8] one seized him by the ear another by the nose, others were catching at his sides and neck, while he was striking right and left sometimes catching a dog and bearing him down in the water until I lost all hope of ever seeing my dogs alive again...[22] I called wildly to the dogs to come*

Custer with the "King of the Forest" killed during the Yellowstone Expedition, September 6, 1873. By William, R. Pywell.

away-almost beseeching them as if they were human, and understood my every word. 'You'll all be killed! You'll all be killed!' was my oft-repeated exclamation as I saw dogs and elk all floundering and fighting in the deep water...[113] You will see on the ears of the buck the prints of their teeth also along his sides where the dogs endeavored to jump up and seize him as he ran. All this time I was on the river bank within twenty yards of the conflict, rifle in hand and calmly watching an opportunity to put a ball in and end the battle and save the lives of my dogs, but so active and mixed up were elk and dogs that for a long time I was unable to aim at the elk without at same time covering a dog, until finally all the dogs concentrated at and about his head when I quickly sent a rifle ball through his loins... and the battle was over...[8] I killed him only a mile and a half from camp, sent for a wagon and carried him entire to camp where a perfect reception was held not only all the officers and men of the 7th gathering around him to look at what everyone pronounced the largest and handsomest elk they had ever seen...

Appropriately named the 'King of the Forest'... his photograph was taken as he lay in front of my tent I being seated in my buckskins near his head... with my unerring rifle thrown carelessly across my lap... with one hand resting on an antler. You may judge of the immense size of the buck when I tell you that as I sat on the ground my head only reached to about half the height of the antlers... He was about fifteen hands high and taller than Dandy, and weighing cleaned eight hundred pounds, with the handsomest pair of antlers I ever saw, and such a beautiful coat... The elk, handsome as he is, and will be, is too large for any private house, unless only the head and neck are taken and even then he is too large for any ordinary sized hall... I think he ought to go where he can be preserved whole... fortunately I had learned during the past year the principles of taxidermy and I have preserved in splendid order not only the antlers head and neck, but the skin and hoofs of the entire animals so they can be mounted 'as natural as life' It is the finest specimen of the elk anywhere in the U.S. so the zoologists accompanying the expedition state... they said that in the east this specimen would be worth several hundred dollars... So I have concluded... to present it to the Audubon Club where it will crown all their collections and be admired by thousands, nothing to equal it, I believe will be found in any other room in the U.S." [22]

His hunting expeditions also captured live a bob cat and a small field mouse who was to live in an ink well on his field desk and fancy climbing up his arm to nest in his hair.

Libbie had taken up sewing while stationed in Kentucky and was proud to send Autie on this campaign wearing the latest stylish fireman's shirt. The bib-front shirt had a large falling collar and was in the General's favorite color of red. Brother Tom was quick to point out it made him a perfect target at the front of the command, Libbie no doubt hoping to collect on his recently purchased Insurance Policy through New York Life. Later she gave the shirts to Armstrong's striker John Burkman for which Autie and Tom accused her of trying to get Burkman shot!

While dozing one afternoon the surveyors returned to camp and Armstrong overheard outside his tent a familiar voice ask, *"Orderly, which is General Custer's tent?"* [15]

Turned out Custer's friend and Civil War antagonist Thomas Rosser was Chief Surveyor for the Northern Pacific Rail Road. Rosser's task was to close the gap in the most cost efficient route between the last stake driven by Civil Engineer John Haydon's survey party and his own work at the mouth of the Powder River. [110]

Equipped with state of the art cartographer maps, government reports, transits, levels and Gunter chains, Rosser fielded a 15 man crew; from instrument men to rodmen, cooks and muleskinners. Traversing for plan and location surveys to in depth topographic studies including forest, fauna and geological information.

"General Rosser has been spending an hour or so with me we have been chatting over our war experiences. Moylan has been sitting by an attentive and interested listener." Rosser took Moylan prisoner once during the war.

"I do not believe we are going to have any serious difficulty with the Indians at least this is General Rosser's opinion. He thinks the expedition too large and unwieldy to performed the desired work promptly, and I agree with him." [22] So far the most difficult problem they'd had to deal with being General Stanley's constant state of drunkenness. On one occasion Stanley going so far as having Armstrong placed under arrest. Rosser successfully interceded and got Stanley to revoke his misconceived sentence. With an apology forth coming within forty eight hours of the time Armstrong was placed in arrest. *"I humbly beg your pardon sir, I am sorry the affair has happened, I not only make this apology to you but if you desire me to do so in the presence of any or all of your officers I will gladly do so."*

After this apology a spirit of friendship grew between the Civil War Veterans and the success of the

Chief Surveyor Thomas Rosser seated with white hat, his team of surveyors and state of the art equipment. Photo courtesy of M. John Lubetkin from 'Jay Cooke's Gamble, The Northern Pacific Railroad, the Sioux and the Panic of 1873'.

Bloody Knife, one of the Custer's favorite scouts.

campaign would follow. Fresh game was plentiful during the expedition but because of the Steamboats that continued to supply the commands, *"I have enjoyed a few very great luxuries today, at dinner on the Josephine when for the first time this season, Sep 10th, I tasted new potatoes and cucumbers, but these were not the greatest. What do you imagine was a greater luxury than these? RAW ONIONS!!!! Even at this great distance I almost tremble when I inform you that I not only had onions for dinner but the Captain of the boat gave me a whole bushel of fine large ones. I supped on RAW ONIONS. I will probably breakfast, lunch and dine on them tomorrow and the next day and the day after ad infinitum until... onions shall be no more. As one by one I dispose of each goodly sized fragment of a huge onion I remark sotto voce 'Go it old fellow, make the most of your liberties, you are on the home stretch now, and school soon commences.' In other words If you intend to eat raw onions now is your only time for 'Missus is comin.'*"[22]

Later while sitting at his desk writing a letter to his wife, Custer was accosted by a belligerent Indian scout who barged into his NPRR Tent gifted to him by Rosser. Quite inebriated, using sign language and broken English the Arikara Scout began complaining to Custer. Getting up from his desk Armstrong popped the Indian twice in the face with his fists and the Indian stumbled and went sprawling out of the tent. Shortly Bloody Knife, leader of the Arikara Scouts appeared to register a complaint. Through sign language he describes that the Indian was almost killed. Armstrong calmly went to his trunk and got out his peace pipe packed and lit it. Motioning for Bloody Knife to sit is his chair. *"Is your man hurt?"*

"Much heap bad-face all blood-may be die." Bloody Knife blurts out in broken English. Custer drew on the pipe then handed it to Bloody Knife who offered it to the four cardinal directions, the earth and heaven before drawing on the stem.

"Listen, I am the big chief here. All these soldiers are under me, and all the chiefs too. You see that?" Bloody knife bowed gravely and grunted. *"And You are the chief of the scouts. All the Indians are under you, because you are a great warrior. You see?"*

Then Bloody Knife drew on the pipe again and grunted his assent. *"No one enters this tent but chiefs and great warriors. Them I am always glad to see. You I am glad to see. You are a chief, a great warrior. You see?"* This time a grunt of unmixed satisfaction. *"When a man comes into my tent without first going to his chief, he dishonors his chief you see? makes a squaw of his chief you see? Throws dirt in his chief's face you see? Says 'you are no chief-you are a squaw-a dog' do you see?"* Bloody Knife handed back the pipe, Custer puffed on it for a few minutes. Bloody Knife sat looking straight ahead then finally as if understanding said, *"How! How!"*

Bloody Knife arose and nodded to Custer then exited his tent. Armstrong heard a frenzy of shouting and yelling, following a painful squawking as Bloody Knife took a buffalo whip to the injured Indian. From that day on Bloody Knife had a great respect and true friendship for Custer and Custer had no more trouble from his Indian scouts. He had shown them respect and the same knowledge of Indian character throughout the rest of his career.[24]

The Yellowstone country was almost as if a Bierstadt painting had come to life. Truly was a case of life imitating art. *"No country in the world so far known to science equals or in any degree compares with this country in the number and character of its petrifactions and fossils. The petrifactions extend to the animal and vegetable kingdoms. No museum in the world can exhibit so rare and curious specimens as are here to be seen. ..I am earnestly engaged in making a collection of specimens of petrifactions, fossils and geological curiosities generally, which will be not only extensive but in the highest degree rare and interesting and to science will be incalculable. Our wagons being light on our return I will be able to transport several boxes of specimens. I already have one nearly filled with a rich collection, and now the part I hope you will approve of is that when collected I propose to present the entire collection to the Ann Arbor University and I will venture to say that if as successful as I hope to be no public or private cabinet will contain so rare and valuable a collection of specimens of the class as that I intend to contribute. Very few scientific men even have ever seen a single petrified tree or a portion of one. What would you think to pass through thousands of acres of petrified trees, some of which are twelve feet in diameter with trunks and branches perfect. Some of these are so perfect in color and grain that without touching them you would regard them only as the natural tree. Some of the officers sat down as they supposed on the trunk of a huge tree what was their astonishment to discover that it was petrified... To me the most interesting fossils so far are those of reptiles or sea fish."* [22]

Allured by these same fossils both the Sutler Baliran and the Veterinarian Honsinger strayed away from the command and were accosted by some Indians. Later their bodies were found pin cushioned by arrows. On the morning of August 4, Armstrong and the cavalry took the advance. Bloody Knife quickly returned claiming he had spotted Indian sign. A small party of Indians had approached during the night, and had left in the direction the command was traveling. Word was sent back to Stanley. Armstrong called a halt to wait for the Infantry to catch up. Pickets were thrown out and the rest of the command lay down to nap. Using his buckskin coat for a pillow, Custer removed his boots, and was soon enjoying this short respite. After about an hour, all were brought awake by the shouts of *"Indians, Indians!"* and firing of their carbines. Custer scooped up his Remington Sporting rifle and, without pulling on his boots yelled, *"Run to your horses, men! Run to your horses!"* About six or so Indians, rode in amongst the men firing at them. Quickly mounting his Kentucky thoroughbred the Boy General got out in front followed by his brother Tom and about a dozen troops. The Indians, using an old decoy ploy slowed to an easy lope trying to lure the troops further. Custer immediately suspected their game telling Tom to watch closely the timber on the left when all at once between 300 and 400 Indians came bursting from the timber, at full speed, yelling and whooping. Wheeling quickly and spurring his mount, Custer galloped back toward Tom, shouting *"Dismount your men! Dismount your men!"* The Indians' determinedly charging in an attempt to overrun them. *"Don't fire, men, till I give the word,"* cautioned Tom Custer. The warriors came on in an unchecked charge. *"Now, men, let them have it!"* cried Tom. Two instantaneous volleys erupted sending several Indians whirling from their mounts. Their line of attack faltered, and soon they were in retreat. A cheer went up followed by a third volley. Now the Indians began to work their way individually through the grass toward the timber where the command, all dismounted, had formed a circular skirmish line to shelter the horses, and make their stand until reinforcements arrived. The Indians kept making every effort to force the defenders onto the plain behind. Continuous firing soon depleted their cartridge boxes and the soldiers' ammunition began to run low

A bold mounted warrior thought to be Crazy Horse made several forays against the line, riding in as close as 200 yards. Everyone had tried to hit him but were unsuccessful. Bloody Knife remarking the next charge would be the Indian's last. Custer told him, through an interpreter, that once the Indian reached the point opposite Bloody Knife to fire at the rider and Armstrong would take out the pony. Custer squatted and leveled his Remington while Bloody Knife steadied his Henry. The two rifles exploded, both Indian and pony fell in a heap. Desperation soon set in when the Sioux attempted to set the grass on fire. *"The Great Spirit will not help our enemies,"* said Bloody Knife. *"See, the grass refuses to burn."* The billowing smoke only acting a beacon. All eyes now turning to the bluffs where coming at full speed, were four separate squadrons with waving banners of the Army's top regiment. The shouts of the beleaguered troopers almost drowning out the familiar clarion of the Sevenths' trumpets putting the hostiles to flight. Estimates of Indian casualties, revealed later equaled almost half of Custer's entire force.

Disgruntled but not defeated these same Indians would later return to agencies *"to receive the provisions and fresh supplies of ammunition which a sentimental government, manipulated and directed by corrupt combinations, insists upon distributing annually."* [114]

Reports of the attack on the railroad workers and the Seventh Cavalry by the Sioux brought about a stop to the NPRR (Northern Pacific Railroad) and a subsequent crash of the stock market.

While still in the field construction of the new Cavalry Post, Fort Abraham Lincoln was near completion.

'Yellowstone Falls'. By Albert Bierstadt.

"My Princess,

...As soon as we can get over and load our wagons we will set out for Lincoln where we expect to arrive in about 12 days from our departure here. By the accompanying order you will see that six companies go to Lincoln and four to Rice. I am to designate the companies and am also to command the six companies at Lincoln. The new quarters are to be completed by the time we arrive... Major Dickey says no quarters in this Department compare to those being built for us, the six troops, and the Commanding officer's house is described as being elegant... one set of field officers quarters at Lincoln and they were said to be for General Custer... the best of pine lumber has been used in all... This settles our location for next winter if not longer and is satisfactory to me... I think you will be warm as the entire house, roof, floors, and walls are enclosed with a layer of inch plank and a layer of that warm paper thus weather boarded on the outside and plastered on the inside, our house is a story higher than the others and as described to me today by Major Dickey it is divided into rooms somewhat after the manner of the new quarters we occupied at Leavenworth that is large double parlors on the right with folding doors, while on the left of the hall are two rooms, my room in the front and the bed room in rear, rooms upstairs and servant rooms in rear, our home faces the river and commands a view of the latter for eight miles with a stretch of timber in sight... The railroad will be completed 27 miles on this side of the river to some valuable coal fields which are to be worked, they will keep railroad communication open with the east all winter and such is the expressed intentions of the R.R. authorities. Is not this all very encouraging, it sounds wonderfully like "Custer luck" I informed Yates today that his troop was going to Lincoln, he was perfectly delighted. I told him because he was writing to Annie and I knew she would be delighted to hear it. I think we will have a charming garrison this winter... The plan of the new post is about as follows... The officers quarters are double sets with separate halls and entrances. They are on higher ground than the men's buildings so that a view of the river is obtained over the men's quarters. There should be three sets of men's quarters instead of four, two companies in each... The officers are hinting strongly in endeavor to ascertain 'who goes where' but thus far none are any the wiser, for the simple reason that... I have not fully decided as to the six troops which I will take to Lincoln this winter but the following I have decided on "B" (Tom is in "B") "C" "F" - probably "A" The other two are still undecided but will be two of the three "E" "G" & "L". This will send to Rice "H" "K" "M" and the odd one of the last named three. Three or four of the officers are going on leaves of from three to six months. Captain Hale - to settle up his father's estate has applied for six months. Captain French has received three or four months leave. McDougal has received six months - he and French only expect to be absent about a month. Still the fact that they have asked for such long leaves has influenced me not a little in assigning them to posts. Lincoln is the first choice of all the officers it would hardly be fair to let an officer who expects to be in the states all winter choose a better post than one who proposes to remain with his troop. With the exception of one officer, I would be glad to have every one of the officers now with me stationed at my post. My relations with them personal and official are extremely agreeable. They are all counting on going with me to Lincoln and I know the Rice party will be disappointed... The steamer Josephine will probably leave here for Lincoln, tomorrow evening or next day, and should reach Lincoln in four or five days so that you should receive this letter in about one week... If no accident occurs we will reach Lincoln before the 1ˢᵗ of October..."

"September 23, '73

My Darling Bunkey

The infantry portion of the garrison is nearly 3/4 of a mile from the cavalry. As soon as we reached here the other day even before I had arrived at the Fort General Carlin sent his orderly to meet me with invitation to at once come to his house. I could not go at the time as I had to see to the dispositions for camp. Another orderly came just at dark with General Carlin's compliments and 'sup-

per is on the table.' So I had to go, and knowing Mrs. Carlin was an army lady and would understand it I made no change in the dress I had been marching in all day, but made my appearance in my famous buckskin suit. I sat down to a delightful supper, ending with a most excellent dish, two in fact, of ice cream. Our house of which I send you a plan, is or will be in my opinion, simply elegant. I like it better than the new quarters we occupied at Leavenworth and they are incomparably superior to any quarters in this Department. The workmen told me yesterday that they could complete the house in one week. The material used is all of the best quality. No cottonwood, but well seasoned pine, the four fireplaces in the large lower rooms are built of the famous Milwaukee brick. The floors are made by first laying down one course of one inch pine planks, on top of this is a layer of that warm paper such as we enjoyed at Yankton, then on top of the paper is a regular floor made of the best quality of pine flooring grooved together. The sides of the house are built similarly, there being a layer of pine plan, then a coating of paper, then regular weatherboarding, then on the inside heavy plaster finished with the ordinary hard finish. The kitchen is large and well lighted with two good large pantries on each side of the hall leading from the kitchen to the dining room. All

the lower rooms are sixteen feet square and eleven and a half feet high, the four guest chambers up stairs are almost as large except cut off by the dormer windows. There are two comfortable servant barns over the kitchen which are reached by a kitchen stairway. The hall is wide and well lighted, one room lacks wardrobes but I intend to see Gen Dandy and endeavor to induce him to put in two large wardrobes. I want two otherwise the number of hooks placed at my disposal will dwindle down until I will find my garments hanging over the back of a broken chair. The parade ground is larger than at any post you have been unless it is Leavenworth. The officers quarters are not close together but almost as wide apart as the distance across the street in front of our house at home. The quarters are all snugly sheltered from the winds by a bluff rising in rear. The men's quarters are just as comfortably constructed as those intended for officers. The post garden here produces the finest quality of vegetables." [22]

Compliments of the Northern Pacific Rail Road Armstrong hopped a train and headed east. Arriving in time to attend the Seventh Re-Union of the Army of the Tennessee in Toledo, Ohio where he and Libbie rubbed elbows with the President, the top Generals of the Army and distinguished guests. All of this before returning to the plains and their new home at Fort Abraham Lincoln. After years of service in the field and The life of Bedouins living in a rag house as Libbie described it, they now had a permanent home. A government home, but for all practical purposes a home they could decorate and entertain from. That is until the night of February 5, 1874 when Libbie awoke to the sound of roaring in the chimney to discover the whole side of room had been blown out and the roof of the house was on-fire. Waking Autie who quickly slipped on his waistcoat and called for the officer of the guard. The bucket brigade was quick in responding, but not as quick as the flames, that seemed to lick the dried wood of the house and completely devour what had been their dream and cherished memories that were lost in the engulfment. *"I had lost silver and linen, and what laces and finery I had,"* lamented Libbie, *"The only loss I mourned, as it was really irreparable, was a collection of newspaper clippings regarding my husband that I had saved during and since the war. Besides these I lost a little wig that I had worn at a fancy-dress ball, made from the golden rings of curly hair cut from my husband's head after the war, when he had given up wearing long locks."* [4]

Temporarily dislocated, it would be but a few months when a new home would emerge from the ashes. Built with their own personal touches and their own designs, it would be in this home that both would remember as their more happier times together.

Custer's first house at their new post of Fort Abraham Lincoln.

"In the Black Hills". By Ralph Heinz.

Into the Pa Ha Sapa

Reeling from the economic collapse of the stock market, all eyes looked to the West, where rumors of a New Gold Strike, bigger than the "California Gold Rush" was about to take place.

"...the Panic of 1873 and severe depression that followed..." wherein *"...Farm prices plunged, jobs were scarce, crime was up, and bankruptcies were far more common. President Ulysses S. Grant faced hard times. He was certainly aware of the calls for opening the Black Hills, not to mention the effect a gold rush would have on the economy."* [115]

Those rumors whether true or pipe dreams of an optimistic society were a temporary distraction from his dysfunctional Presidency.

"I am inclined to think that the occupation of this region of the country is not necessary to the happiness and prosperity of the Indians," wrote Secretary of the Interior Columbus Delano, *"And as it is supposed to be rich in minerals and lumber it is deemed important to have it freed as early as possible from Indian occupancy."* [116]

Explicit terms in the 1868 Laramie Treaty forbade *"...no persons except those designated herein ... shall ever be permitted to pass over, settle upon, or reside in the territory described in this article."* [117] Yet in total disregard of that agreement, General Philip H. Sheridan cut a military order authorizing the formation of a column of reconnaissance that turned out to be the largest scientific expedition ever mounted on this continent. [118]

Harboring seeds of jealousy, but climbing on the "GarryOwen" Band Wagon of the Country's Boy General and recent bestselling author, Grant elected to launch The Seventh Cavalry and the Man they called G. A. C. "Jack" once more into the breach. Congress even went as far as making it official and Armstrong was awarded his Brevet Title of Major General and was actually able to draw that pay during his trek into the sacred hills the Lakota called the "Pa Ha Sapa."

Slightly delayed in order to arm the troops with the new Springfield .45-55 Carbines and Colt Single Action revolvers, the command moved out from Fort Abraham Lincoln, on July 2, 1874 to the sixteen piece Regimental Band's rendition of "The Girl I Left Behind Me." The Band was followed by Lonesome Charley Reynolds and Bloody Knife leading the retinue of nearly sixty scouts and guides. Augmenting the column was three Gatling Guns, a Rodman three inch Field piece, over a 100 supply wagons carrying two month's stock of provisions for ten troops of the Seventh Cavalry, and one company each of the Seventeenth and Twentieth Infantries and a herd of 300 cattle.[122]

Members of the Black Hill's expedition. G. A. Custer sits on a white horse in the left foreground.

The detachment comprised more than 1,000 men, a Stereo Optic Photographer and one black woman, Sarah Campbell, cook and first non-Indian woman to enter the Black Hills. The scientific corps was made up of a geologist and his assistant, a naturalist, a botanist, a medical officer, a topographical engineer, a zoologist and a civilian engineer along with two practical miners, Horatio N. Ross and William T. McKay, also attached to the scientific corps; Fred Grant, the President's son was again on hand acting as a personal aide to Custer and Armstrong's brother-in-law James Calhoun this time the Adjutant of the Regiment. Younger brother Boston Custer as well drawing on the payroll as a herder. Tom and Autie were able to add a great deal of mischief to this family outing by playing the usual Custer pranks on poor Bos. Presenting him with several smooth stones one evening, Tom explained to Boston if he'd keep them in water for a few days they'd soften and become the highest quality "Sponge Stones" even better than the sponges harvested from the ocean. After several days of carefully transporting the stones immersed in the water of his tin cup Bos realized his brother was putting him on and gave up tending and nursing stones that would never be anything but familiar rocks![122]

"Prospect Valley, Dakota, 12 miles from Montana line, July 15, 1874.

My darling Sunbeam
We are making a halt of one day at this beautiful spot in order to rest the animals and give the men an opportunity to rest themselves... We have marched through an exceedingly interesting and beautiful country. And we are now encamped in the most beautiful valley we have seen thus far... I directed Colonel Ludlow to name it Prospect Valley. Three days ago we reached... Ludlow's... cave... It was found to be about four hundred feet long... its walls and top were covered by inscriptions and drawings of animals and prints of hands and feet in the rocks. I think this was all the work of Indians at an early day, although I cannot satisfactorily account for drawings of ships found there... No Indians were seen from the time we left Lincoln until day before yesterday when about 20 were seen by Captain McDougall near the column. They scampered off as soon as discovered. Yesterday we came to where they had slept. Captain Moylan who was on rear guard duty saw about 25 following our trail. Signal smokes were also sent up all around us by the Indians yesterday afternoon, and Indians were seen watching us after we reached camp but no hostile demonstration has been made and none may be made, as some of our Indian guides say the signals may be intended to let the village know where we are so that they may keep out of our way. We expect to reach the base of the Black Hills in three days. Professor Winchell and Mr. Grinnell discovered yesterday the fossil remains of an animal belonging to some extinct race, this animal was larger in life than the largest elephant... There has not been a single card party or a drunken officer since we left Lincoln, although I am satisfied that if I once played cards and invited the officers to join there would be playing every night. Sandy is delighted with the 7th Cavalry and says there is no cavalry regiment will compare with it unless perhaps it is the 4th.

The 7th Cavalry Officers on the Black Hills expedition. August 13, 1874. G. A. Custer reclines in the center of the photograph.

"String of Pearls". Custer's 110 wagons snake their way through the Black Hill's Castle Creek Valley.

Colonel Tilford's health is excellent and he enjoys the trip very much. He says he thinks more highly of the 7ᵗʰ than he ever did before, our mess is a decided and most gratifying success...We breakfast at 4 every morning. Every day I invite some officer to dine with us. Yesterday we had Mr. Wallace. I ride at the head of the column and keep inside our lines all the time, although it is a great deprivation to me not to go outside and hunt...But I received my orders from my commanding officer before starting and I am going to try to render strict obedience. In looking for a road I

sometimes get a mile or perhaps two ahead of the command but I always have seventy or eighty men with me and I intend to take in addition to above two companies with me and have no intention of getting beyond sight and hearing of the main column. I keep men in front of me all the time and Indian scouts well out to the front and flanks. I have killed six antelope at the head of the column. Bos also killed one. Sandy Forsyth has just been reading his report to General Sheridan of our trip so far in which he speaks of Lieutenant Wallace as a fine active young officer of

One of Custer's many campsites during the expedition.

great promise...I have told you that which you most desired to know, that I was well and have been so and that I do not expose myself. As I write Cardigan is sleeping on the edge of my bed, Tuck at the head...I need not tell my little durl how constantly and unceasingly I have missed her from her place at my side. She knows all that without being told. But she may not know that I have never felt the loss of her presence more than I do and have done since leaving Lincoln. I look forward with such pleasant anticipations to our future which now seems so brimful of happiness in prospect. I never was more completely furnished for the field than I am now. I am not certain whether I will be able to send back more scouts hereafter or not. This mail is to be carried by two Rees, Bull Bear and Skunks Head, - Bloody Knife is doing splendidly on this trip. There is not a single man on the sick report in the entire command, a fact which the Medical officer regards as unprecedented. We will move into the valley of the Little Missouri tomorrow and probably follow that stream to the Black Hills...I will say bye bye and ask God to keep my darling safe and well and grant us a fast and speedy reunion. Captain Smith is earning praises from everyone by his admirable management of the trains. You may judge of the fine country here passed over by the fact that our mules and beef herd have actually improved since we left Lincoln...We have travelled 227-1/2 miles - and in a straight line we are 170 miles from Lincoln. Our bearing from Lincoln is south 62 degrees west. This leaves at 9 p.m. Oh if I could only get home nights I wouldn't mind riding all day. The Indians have a new name for me but I will not commit it to paper." [22] It was the endearing term *"Hard Ass"* for his celibacy of the saddle, which Bloody Knife attributed *"...no other man could ride all night and never sleep."* [120]

Temperatures during the daylight hours often exceeded the 100 degrees mark, with little or no shade on the prairie, the troops suffered from sunburns and dehydration. Heat exhaustion finally took its toll on the troops, almost as if they were being cremated alive; Private John Cunningham becoming the expedition's first casualty, dying from dysentery. He would be joined beneath the soil by Trooper James Turner shot by William Rollins in a dispute over a horse.

By July 18, the expedition reached the Belle Fourche River. Two days later entering the foothills from the north and turning east into the heart of the mysterious "Pa Ha Sapa" now dubbed by the Sioux "The Thieves Road."

William H. lllingworth, the Stereographer who had been contracted to supply six sets of printed pictures from the expedition, went to work setting up his bulky equipment to capture a string of canvas topped wagons stretching through the valley. The best ambulance being reserved as a wildlife menagerie, filled with owls, rabbits, rattlesnakes and interesting mineral deposits. [117]

With a hammer and chisel William Ludlow carved "Custer 74" into the carboniferious limestone of Inyan Kara Mountain reaching an altitude of over 6600 feet. From this height Armstrong could observe the prairie in flames to the south and west. The scouts believed the fire had been set by hostile Sioux to deter the column's progress.

Continuing east the next day the broken landscape opened into a wide meadow proclaimed Floral Valley. *"Every step of our march was amidst flowers of the most exquisite colors and perfume. So luxuriant in growth are they*

Ludlow's Inscription 'Custer '74'.
By Lyle Reedstorm.

that the men plucked them without dismounting from the saddle! (Some belonged to new or unclassified species.) It was a strange sight to glance back at the advancing column of Cavalry and behold the men with beautiful bouquets in their hands, while the head-gear of their horses was decorated with wreathes of flowers fit to crown a queen of May."[44]

Climbing to the top of a high shelf Felix Vinitieri and his band serenaded the command with, "Mocking Bird," "Artist Life," "The Blue Danube," "Trovatore," and of course "GarryOwen."[115]

Castle Creek was arrived at on July 26, the report of smoke was investigated and the discovery of a recently abandoned village allowed the scouts to ride forward at a rapid rate overtaking a small band of twenty five Sioux Indians fleeing under the leadership of an old chief named One Stab. Sitting with the Long Haired Chief over a pipe of peace, Custer promised security if One Stab would lead them into the interior of the Hills. It was agreed. Passing

a large mound of Elk Antlers, One Stab indicated that this was big medicine. When questioned who had gathered them? The old chief explained they had been there a long time no one knowing who'd put the antlers there, quite probably the creator.

It was to the Pa Ha Sapa that the Indians returned to each summer to cut the long lodge poles for their teepees that could not be found elsewhere, and to commune with Wakan Tanka, the Great Spirit who had made this oasis in the prairie for them.[121]

Their services no longer needed, Pa Haska "The Long Hair" gave them their parole. Bloody Knife instantly became incensed retorting, *"General Custer big chief-White warriors brave-We have seen the chief and his warriors fight the Sioux on the Yellowstone last year and know them to be very brave-We are the chief's friends-The Sioux are the chief's enemies-They are also our enemies-They want to get our scalps-They want to burn the Ree and the white warriors at the stake-The chief of the whites ... captured 27 Sioux-He... let them*

Custer sits with three of his Arikara scouts and an unidentified orderly possibly Private Noonan?

Engraving showing a time of relax during the expedition. Baseball was a very popular game played by troopers.

go-This was wrong-It was wrong to the Rees-It was wrong to the white warriors-It was wrong to the chief himself-The Ree warriors felt bad-They ...(now will return)... to Fort Lincoln without a single scalp-They had told their squaws that they would bring their belts full of scalps-Now they...(will)...be liars...(Bloody Knife hopes)...that the chief would never do this again." [115]

On July 31ˢᵗ, the wagon train reached Harney Peak in an open area east of the present town of Custer, just as he had scaled the 6,000-foot Inyan Kara a week before, now Custer set off to conquer an even higher peak estimated at 7,244 feet the highest spot in the Hills. Armstrong and William Ludlow, the Scientific officer along with several other men climbed to the top of mountain.

Late in the afternoon, after a day of struggling across heavily forested slopes and gorges, the small party arrived at the base of Harney's Peak, not to be defeated the adventurous Custer continued to climb on. When he reached the summit the names of the six explorers were recorded on a small piece of notepaper *"Gen. G. A. Custer, Gen. G. A. Forsyth, Col. Wm. Ludlow, W. H. Wood, A. D. Donaldson, N. H. Winchell, July 31, 1874;"* stuffed into an empty cartridge shell and pounded into a crevice of the granite barrier. [115]

While the climbing excursion was taking place the first of several baseball games was played for the first time in the Hills while the prospectors triumphantly announced the discovery of gold on French Creek.

While the cat's away the mice would play, Colonel Tilford along with Fred Benteen organized a champagne party hosting Fred Grant who along with the rest of the ensemble nursed hangovers the following morning. Unbeknownst to the General who had arrived from his climb in the late hours of the night, making plans for a late morning and saving face for the once robust partiers slowly crawled from their bivouacs.

Word of the discovery would be sent in official dispatches, along with the mailbag containing Custer's descriptive letter to Libbie *"...gold has been found at several places, and it is the belief of those who are giving their attention to this subject that it will be found in paying quantities. I have on my table forty or fifty small particles of pure gold... most of it obtained today from one pail full of earth... We marched forty five miles today in a southerly direction from Harney's Peak and are now encamped on the South Fork of the Sheyenne River about ninety miles from Laramie. Reynolds leaves us here..."* [22]

Reversing the horse's shoes, Reynolds picked up a mailbag stenciled *"Black Hills Express, Charley Reynolds, manager. Connecting with all points east, west, north, south. Cheap rates, quick transit, safe passage. We are protected by the Seventh Cavalry."*

Reynolds made the 90-mile ride to Fort Laramie in four nights, hiding during the day to escape detection by hostile Indians and bringing the electrifying news to the outside world.[117]

Private James King and Sergeant Charles Sempker were the final casualties of the campaign, both succumbing to chronic dysentery and being interred on the trail.

"Bear Butte, Aug. 15, 1874, 8 P.M.

My darling Sunbeam
And now that we have been in and through the Black Hills I have the proud satisfaction of knowing that the expedition has proved a great success far exceeding the expectations of the most sanguine, and I know that my superior officers will be surprised and gratified at the extent and thoroughness of my explorations. Captain Smith has proved himself on this trip the best Quartermaster I have ever had with me in the field and so say we all of us. Our photographer has obtained a complete set of magnificent stereoscopic views of Black Hill scenery so I will not allude to the beautiful scenery until I can review it with you by and of the photographs. I send you one of his stereoscopic views which will show that at last I have reached the highest rung on the hunters ladder of fame I have killed my grizzly after a most exciting hunt and combat. Colonel Ludlow, Bloody Knife and Private Noonan 7th C are with me in the group we constituted the hunting party. Is not the picture superb. The grizzly was eight feet in height. I have his claws. (Sandy stands near my tent in the picture.) The scouts are on their ponies in front of my tent, the mail

Champagne Party.

is waiting for me. We will reach Lincoln Aug 31ˢᵗ Everybody is well and I am happy in the prospect of seeing my little durl so soon... No Indians have been seen but I intend to be careful until the end of the trip."

Custer's 3,500-word dispatch to General Alfred H. Terry at his St. Paul headquarters waxed poetically about the Black Hills. But it was the line "Gold in the Grass roots" that caught the attention of the country and gave birth to one of the most fascinating mining towns in the old west, the lawless and reprehensible Deadwood, Dakota Territory.[117]

To the martial aires of "GarryOwen" the expedition returned to Fort Lincoln on August 30 having traveled 883 miles in 60 days.

News of gold reached the east in unprecedented speed, the New York Herald printing: *"It is inconsistent with our civilization and with common sense to allow the Indian to roam over a country as fine as that around the Black Hills, preventing its development in order that he may shoot game and scalp his neighbors. That can never be. This region must be taken from the Indian even as we took Pennsylvania and Illinois."*[119]

Innumerable prospecting parties soon flooded into Bismarck. Many claiming the Army owed them protection. Custer spent a lot of time in his study, writing articles for "Galaxy" and "Turf, Field and Farm." It wasn't unusual that he would take a prolonged interest in his poultry, hiding in the chicken coop to avoid unwanted visitors to Fort Lincoln. That fall he studied Napoleon's campaigns-especially Napier's

His Hunter's Highest Round of Fame. On the 1874 expedition Custer again indulged in his passion for the hunt.

six volume "War in the Peninsula." That part of Spain resembling the West so familiar to Armstrong.[51]

His Study became his inter-sanctum, *"He filled it with the trophies of the chase. Over the mantle a buffalo's head plunged, seemingly, out of the wall...The head of the first grisly that he had shot, with its open jaws and great fang-like teeth, looked fiercely down on the pretty, meek-faced jack rabbits on the mantel... Several antelope head were on the walls... A sand-hill crane... A mountain eagle, a yellow fox... Over his desk, claiming a perch on a pair of deer antlers, was a great white owl... in one corner... a collection of pistols, hunting knives, Winchester and Springfield rifles, shotguns and carbines, and even an old flintlock... From antlers above hung sabers, spurs, riding whips, gloves and caps, field glasses, the map case, and the great compass used on marches. One of the sabers was remarkably large... there was doubtless no other arm in the service that could wield it... a Damascus blade... from some Spanish ancestor... Do not draw me without cause; Do not sheathe me without honor."*

It was to this room the Great Chiefs would come for council. They would sit on furs and buffalo robes, smoke the pipe and talk of days long past. Armstrong knew the days of the free roamers soon to be coming to an end. The plight of the Redman often in conflict with the needs or wants of modern civilization. Even then overtures of purchase for the Black Hills had been rejected by the Lakota. Confined to rudimentary reservations, they were forced to eat their dogs and ponies to keep from starving when promised goods were late in coming west. *"The suffering among the Indians was very great...and touched the quick sympathies of my husband,"* wrote Libbie Custer. *"He was a sincere friend of the reservation Indian."* [4]

The winter of '74-'75 found temperatures dropping to below freezing. Hunkered in the reservations were many of the Summer Roamers. Those who had fought the Seventh up on the Yellowstone, stood in line for government handouts. Their Hudson Bay Blankets wrapped around them in a fashion hardly distinguishing male from female, one brave from another. Sequestered in the Trader's Store at Standing Rock, Charley Reynolds waited out the storm wrapped in a trade blanket like the others. Familiar with the language of the Lakota, he overheard the haughty confession of a warrior named Rain-in-the-Face in the deaths of Augustus Baliran and

John Honsinger during the summer of '73. When that information reached Fort Lincoln, Armstrong quickly dispatched Tom Custer and George Yates to Standing Rock with a detail of fifty men to arrest Rain-In-The-Face and bring him back to Lincoln.

Standing for hours Tom was only able to identify the warrior in question when he dropped his blanket momentarily, revealing a repeating rifle that Tom wrenched from him in his apprehension and removal from the store. All happened in a matter of moments, but the departure from Standing Rock grew intense and bloodshed would have ensued if the Big Bellies had not interceded staying the young warriors from reprisal. Long Hair's interrogation proved fruitless at first. Rain-In-The-Face eventually told all before being put in the guard house where he remained for the rest of the winter. By spring he had secured his escape vowing that he would cut the heart of "Little Hair" out and eat it! [122]

'Lieutenant Colonel G. A. Custer in his study'.
Engraving by Albert Berghaus.

G. A. Custer from the Payette Collection.
Monroe Evening News.

From the Prairie to Politics

"Let Us Have Peace" the campaign slogan for Ulysses S. Grant's candidacy for the White House was all but forgotten by the end of his second term of office. Any hope of a third term bid had been dashed in the overall corrupt administration's eight years of scandals. In March of 1876, Congressman Joseph Blackburn from Kentucky broke the Post Trader Scandals. Subpoenas were drafted and sent to military officers on the frontier. As the expedition against the Sioux was originally scheduled to leave Fort Abraham Lincoln on April 6, 1876, Custer was reluctant to get involved.

On March 15, Custer was summoned to Washington to testify before Hiester Clymer's Congressional Committee Hearings. Clymer was after big game on a hot trail.[79]

Seems Secretary of War William Belknap and Caleb P. Marsh were in league in a corrupt scheme to charge the Indian Traders exorbitant prices to maintain their franchises at Military Posts and Indian Reservations in the West.

Custer testified on March 29, that Post Traders were required to pay $5,000 per year to keep their franchises that brought in between $25,000 to $75,000 annually. S. A. Dickey, sutler at Fort Abraham Lincoln was charged with violating Revenue Laws when he sold liquor to the Indians and was quickly replaced by Robert Seip who immediately inflated prices to cover a third of his profits ear marked for Secretary Belknap and the President's Brother Orville Grant.

Belknap's brother-in-law, J. M. Hedrick and E. W. Rice, a claim-agent also purportedly received a portion of the profit from Seip. Although hearsay, Custer's testimony implicated Rice of receiving $5,000 in kick backs from the deal. Rice publicly denied the claim calling Armstrong a bald faced liar. Taking umbrage to such accusation, Custer caned him that same evening on G street in Washington D. C.[44]

In addition to Seip, Belknap was accused of shaking down John Evans, Post Trader at Fort Sill for the sum of $24,450. Custer was told by Evans that Marsh extorted $12,000 from him alone in order that Evans might keep his franchise at Sill.[123] Another Post Trader, William Harmon unable to pay was told he had twenty four hours to accept or reject Orville Grant's offer to buy him out.

In order to meet these outrageous fees traders all along the frontier were forced to pass the cost on to their customers. Military families on fixed incomes could not afford to purchase items from the traders and resorted to buying goods off post until an order was sent from Secretary of War Belknap that all purchases must be made from the Post Sutler. Post traders were known to stop and inspect wagons they suspected had purchased goods off the military reservation at half the trader's prices.[79]

Successfully engineering to get General of the Army William Tecumseh Sherman out of the country from November 1871 to September 1872, Belknap had free rein in his elaborate plan to control the purse strings of the Military and the Interior Department costs to the reservations.

From 1866 to 1876 the cost to the United States Government for the Reservation System rose from an annual budget of $1Million to $20 Million per year. Even though the prices went up the annuities promised to the Indians never arrived at the reservations. The broken promises and dishonest Indian Agents dashed any hope of appeasement, *"The Great Father may choose only good men, as you say,"* Running Antelope told Custer. *"And they may be good men when they leave Washington, but by the time they get to us they are damned thieves, and we would like a change."*[124] The same unscrupulous agents were not adverse to selling illegal firearms to the Indians as well.

In a letter from John Smith to Custer in February of 1874, Smith explained the magnitude of corruption, *"Fully three-fourths of all Indians enumerated are Hostiles, the bitter ones being old men"*.

"You can count on each lodge furnishing one and one-half warriors, able-bodied, two-thirds well armed. Fully half the young men have pistols-one or more, exclusive of other arms. About half the warriors remaining at the Agencies have repeating rifles, Winchesters and all others have breech-loaders. I have known Indians at White River Agency to have 3,000 rounds of ammunition for a single gun."[15]

Captain J. S. Poland of the Six Infantry at Standing Rock Agency reported excessive sales of Winchesters and over 150,000 rounds of ammunition distributed to the agency Indians, far exceeding the warranted needs for hunting and killing of their allotted government beef. These claims not only fell on deaf ears, they did not go beyond the Office of the Secretary of War.

"...the Indian Department, which, seeing that its wards are determined to fight, is equally determined

President Ulysses S. Grant.

that there shall be no advantage taken, but that the two sides shall be armed alike; proving, too, in this manner the wonderful liberality of our Government, which not only is able to furnish its soldiers with the latest improved style of breech-loaders to defend themselves, but equally able and willing to give the same pattern of arms to their common foe. The only difference is, that the soldier, if he loses his weapon, is charged double price for it; while to avoid making any such charge against the Indian, his weapons are given him without conditions attached." [73]

Yet this was only the tip of the iceberg. When 8,000 bushels of corn was sent to Fort Lincoln in bags marked "Indian Bureau," General Custer refused to accept the corn, until an order from Belknap forced him to do so.

The corn in the mis-marked bags undoubtedly having been purchased by the government twice.

Flour earmarked for the reservations ended up in warehouses in Bismarck and sold illegally to prospectors headed for the Black Hills.

The sutler at Fort Berthold Reservation, J. W. Raymond paid $1,000 to Orville Grant for his appointment. In order to recoup his loss he took in large amounts of flour and then claimed that flour perished in a fire and petitioned the government for replacements. At the same time purchases were made of flour from that area by settlers and citizens along the river, purchased from steam vessels contracted to deliver government provisions for the Reservation Indians.

When a delegation of Indians arrived at Fort Lincoln with a request for food, Custer contacted Secretary Belknap for permission to distribute some of the military stores to the Indians until such time provisions arrived at the reservation. Belknap denied the application.

By spring the Indians faced a decision, remain on the reservations and starve or return to the frontier and their old way of life.

Reservations began to see a mass exodus and quickly an order went out to the absent tribes from the Government, *"Return to the Reservations by January 31, 1876 or be deemed hostile and turned over to the Military."*

When April 10, rolled around Custer had hopes of heading west. Dashing off a note to Libbie, he maintained his enthusiasm of breaking free of the Hearings. *"My Darling Sunbeam: I calculate on one week more here. Should I be detained longer I should give up all thought of a summer campaign and send for my Bunkey. Many would rejoice at a summer in the east. But not I.* [15] *If you get an opportunity to see Bloody Knife and you had better send for him as he will be delighted. Tell him I have not forgotten my promise to him and today I visited the Great father*

Secretary of War William Belknap.

and told him what a brave and faithful friend Bloody Knife had proved himself and the Great father at my request has given me a handsome silver medal to carry to Bloody Knife as recognition of his valuable services. The medal is of solid silver. I am going to have Bloody Knife's name engraved upon it." [22]

On April 18, he also testified in support of the Democrats before the Banning Committee. Unable to substantiate rumors that Major Lewis Merrill had accepted bribes from the State of South Carolina or that Merrill's denials were false, Custer's testimony only created hard feelings between himself and Merrill.[125]

After Belknap's indictment Custer was excused and released as none of the charges against Belknap relied upon his sole testimony. On April 20, instead of returning immediately to Fort Lincoln, he headed to Philadelphia to visit the Centennial Exposition, then traveled to New York to meet with his publishers. While there he received a summons from the Senate, possibly instigated by President Grant.

Returning to Washington on April 21, Custer found himself the target of a campaign of vilification by the Republican Press; accused of perjury and disparagement of brother officers. General Sherman realizing the need to get Custer out of Washington, asked the new Secretary of War,

Alphonso Taft, to write a letter requesting Custer's release so he could return to Fort Lincoln to head up the expedition against the Sioux. President Grant forbade the letter to be sent and ordered Taft to appoint another officer to lead the campaign. Brig. Gen. Alfred Terry determined that there we no available officers of appropriate rank, was told by Sherman to appoint himself, while a stunned Custer realizing he was no longer in command, approached the impeachment managers and secured his own release. General Sherman now advised Custer not to leave before personally meeting with The President. Custer arranged for Colonel Rufus Ingalls to request a private meeting, but after several days of waiting outside the Oval Office, Grant refused to see him. The President considered Custer's testimony to be an all out attack on his and his administrations character and left him to cool his heels in the anteroom.[79] On the evening of May 3, an anxious and impatient Custer caught a train for Chicago.

His brief but pleasant stop in Monroe allowed for a shorter than normal haircut at Bernard Verhoeven's Barbershop. Verhoeven claimed Custer often would let his hair grow until he could come home to Monroe and have him cut it. Custer's hair was light and wavy, worn longer than anyone else at the time. Verhoeven's was the most popular barbershop in the

A short haircut for G. A. Custer. By Ken Smith.

area and kept between 600 to 700 personalized shaving mugs for his customers; the General's mug was kept on the shelf with his name and image embossed on it. That day while Custer was in the back room, Bernard asked his nephew Autie Reed, *"What are you going to do while your uncle is out fighting the Indians?"*

"Oh, I'm going along to see the fun." [126] *"He stopped here from the morning train until evening only,"* Emanuel Custer remembered of the General's brief visit, *"...He seemed in good spirits as ever...I remember he told me that Bloody Knife had sent him word he was going to take his scalp, and he laughed as he said it."* [127]

The following morning General Sherman sent a telegram to General Sheridan ordering him to intercept Custer and hold him until further orders. Sheridan was also informed to proceed with the expedition against the Sioux; Major Reno commanding the Seventh in Custer's absence. Sherman, Sheridan, and Terry all wanted Custer at the helm, but had no choice but to support The President. Sherman wrote Terry: *"Custer's political activity has compromised his best friends here, and almost deprived us of the ability to serve him."*

When Brig. Gen. Terry met Custer in St. Paul, Minnesota on May 6 *"(Custer) with tears in his eyes, begged for my aid. How could I resist it?"*

Picking up pen and paper in a most humble way Custer began to write, *"To His Excellency The President, through Military Channels: I have seen your order transmitted through the general of the army, directing that I not be permitted to accompany the expedition about to move against the Indians. As my entire regiment forms part of the proposed expedition, and as I am senior officer of the regiment on duty in this department, I respectfully, but most earnestly request that, while not allowed to go in command of the expedition, I may be permitted to serve with my regiment in the field. I appeal to you as a soldier to spare me the humiliation of seeing my regiment march to meet the enemy and I not share in its dangers."* [9]

Terry wrote the President explaining he did not intend to question Grant's orders *"...but if these reasons do not forbid it, Lieutenant Colonel Custer's services would be very valuable with his regiment."*

The President already under pressure from the Democratic Press for his treatment of Custer, began to have concern that should the Sioux campaign fail, he would be seen as an obstruction to the recommendations of his Generals. He now had little choice but to relent.

Suggesting Armstrong should restrain himself in the future, General Sherman wrote Terry *"Advise Custer to be prudent, and not to take along any news-*

paper men who always work mischief and to abstain from any personalities in the future."[128]

On May 8, Custer was informed at Department Headquarters in the 1850 Administration building on Fort Snelling that he would lead the 7th, but only under Terry's direct supervision.

An exuberant Custer while on his way to the Metropolitan Hotel ran into General Terry's chief engineer, Captain William Ludlow, telling him the worm had turned and now he'd gotten his command back, he would shortly *"swing clear of Terry"* just as he'd done Stanley, the first chance he got. Although this story is unsubstantiated, critics have used this to conclude that Custer was to blame for the coming disaster by seeking to claim all the victory for himself.[44]

Equivalent to a policeman, Custer's job was to keep peace and order. He'd had no problem with the Indians retaining their own lands or for that manner being placed on a reservation. But that was not his decision to make. His superiors in Washington now ordered him to round up the hostile tribes and if necessary forcibly return them to the reservations.

He was a soldier, a good soldier and despite popular belief did not disobey orders.

Armstrong's instructions were to pursue the hostiles and round them up and return them to the reservations by the end of summer. The War Department suggested approximately 800 warriors were in the field. In the Summer of 1876 the Indian estimates may not have been completely accurate; the "something" they couldn't put a figure on was the charismatic influence wielded by Tatanka Iyotanka. Sitting Bull, Spiritual Leader of the Non-Treaty Lakota called for a gathering in the Yellowstone Country. The Medicine Man may or may not have known what this Summer had in store for his people, but he soon would.

'Sitting Bull'.
By Harley Brown.

"Son of the Morning Star". By C. Gómez.

To the Little Big Horn and Glory

The pitter patter of rain drops on canvas mimicked the Lakota Medicine Man's death rattle. Sitting Bull had never signed a treaty and now sent word to all the nations; Come out of the reservations. Gather this summer for one last time, before the old ways are gone forever.[129]

Just a few months from our Country's 100th Birthday and already the excitement and momentum was building. Armstrong spoke of wonders he had experienced at the Philadelphia Centennial. International exhibits in manufacturing, the arts, products of agriculture and mining; horticulture and science. From sewing machines to the Centennial's Centerpiece the Corliss Engine, the most powerful machine built to date. Over 274,000 people walked the grounds daily, marveling at the Industrial Revolution. The United States had become a world power. And although Armstrong was amused by it, he felt Alexander Graham Bell's invention would never replace the written word in communication. To some the world was shrinking.

The east was latticed with rails of iron and networks of paved streets and cosmopolitan amusements. Over 46 million people were bursting at the seams and eager to venture into the frontier.

Bismarck remained the end of the Northern Pacific Line. *"After Fort Lincoln, pilgrim you were on your own."* The military for now was a necessity, recalcitrant tribes still roamed at will, and *"Go West Young Man"* (said by John B. L. Soule though popularly attributed to Horace Greely) was the theme of the day.

"Dear Sister, ...We expect to go out after Sitting Bull and his cut throats, and if old Custer gets after him he will give him the fits for all the boys are spoiling for a fight..." (Blacksmith Henry Bailey, Company I, 7th U. S. Cavalry).[130]

Lightening illuminated the company streets of the tent city erected near the flat area just south of the commissary, within 2 miles of the post. For the Seventh Cavalry the wet spring had delayed their departure; and this had worked to their advantage;

The author and his wife Sandy re-create May 17, 1876.

distributed to posts and forts across the country, the Seventh was now being called together for the first time since the Regiment's creation. Two companies of the 7th Cavalry arrived at Fort Abraham Lincoln on May 5, and went into camp, they were soon joined by all the Cavalry and the Infantry assigned to the campaign who shook out their tentage. It had rained on and off through May 15, and that had contributed to their delay in order to dry out the canvas. While on Post the tents were set up in rows with company streets, on campaign these same soldiers would throw up their half shelters upon arrival into camp in any hap-hazard fashion. Usually the Troop that was packed and ready first would take the advance and lead out the regiment.[131]

Anxious and unable to sleep Armstrong sat up reading from a novel and underlined the passage: *"I have faith in my own fortunes, and I believe I shall conquer in the end."* It was the last book he would read, from a three-volume set "Her Dearest Foe." The author's last name was Alexander.

All at once, Libbie was jolted awake, having had a nightmare she described as a Cheyenne Brave holding a bloody blond scalp aloft. She reached over and ran her fingers through Armstrong's closely shorn locks. Now if she could only convince him not to wander too far ahead of the column.

At 4:00 AM on May 17, both she and Autie, were brought wide awake by the sound of reveille. At 5:00 AM "General" was sounded and the tents were

Custer's buckskins undoubtedly are one of his most significant trademarks and symbolic of his deep identification with the western way of life. The Jacket and pants in the middle -same as the sombrero and gauntlets- are faithful replicas of the ones worn by the General at the Little Big Horn. The jacket was tailored according to period photographs and reports while the pants, made to be used with tall riding boots, are an exact replica of a surviving specimen. Custer was naked and stripped of all his belongings when found after the battle and none of these garments have since emerged. This buckskin would arguably be similar to the first one Custer had tailored in 1869; probably by Saddler Sergeant Jeremiah Finley, who may have produced also the second and surviving original jacket on the right. A fourth buckskin coat reported to have belonged to GAC sold on Ebay in 2005. Once

owned by Colonel Raymond Vietzen the elaborately beaded coat may have been sewn by Helen Soos Lewis, the half-Blackfoot wife of Robert Jackson one of Custer's Scouts during the 1876 Campaign. Only three of these jackets are recorded as they appear in this spread; all of them sporting fringes and military buttons. The one on the left is also an original piece although not appearing in any known period photograph. Unlike the others –both buckskins- this one was made from cowhide. It has been suggested that Custer, being of superstitious nature, would have liked donning old buckskins in campaign rather than newly made ones to prevent bad luck. Notwithstanding a simple demand for some comfort would seem a more reasonable explanation, especially when considering the long and exhausting rides usually preceding any battle during the Indian wars...

Mark Kellogg, Reporter for the Bismarck Tribune.

Boston Custer.

brought down and gear packed. By 7:00 AM all were in saddle and the procession was headed toward the fort. The Scouts led off the command with their

weird and melancholy singing, this kept up as the column swung past Laundress Row. The laundresses were tending to their sheets and white shirts hanging

Custer's Revolver Found at Little Big Horn?

1869 Tranter Bull Dog which hammer and other parts are unfortunately missing so that the firing pin mark cannot be tested.

Tom Custer's English pistols are inscribed on the ivory grips and if this gun was ever so inscribed, it would also have been on the ivory. Note that the gun is quite nicely engraved in very fine English scroll work.

When Mr. Aplan first acquired the gun he was offered quite a bit of money for it but as to this day, he is not prepared to sell it. According with a former Superintendent of the Custer Battle Field at that time, if they ever found a lead bullet from a .450 English pistol, they would try to match it up to this gun. The bullet would be unique as so would the rifling in this gun. As they have only metal detected a small portion of the battlefield as to this date, it may be some time, if ever before they find a bullet.

Mr Jim Aplan has been an avid collector/dealer for over 70 years and has owned many Custer artifacts, including the famous 1866 Winchester carbine that matched a cartridge found on the battlefield and sold for several hundred thousand dollars. He is also the owner of this revolver that was sold several years ago to a scrap iron dealer in Nebraska by some Sioux Indians from the Pine Ridge Indian Reservation in South Dakota. Mr. Aplan heard about it and chased it down and bought the piece, fully aware of the story and wondering where the Indians would have gotten such a gun. That it could be the Custer's gun is somewhat open to speculation but there is no doubt that it was a fine piece in its day. It is a Model

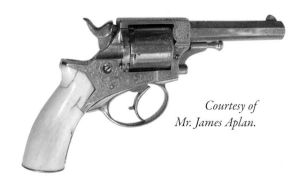

Courtesy of Mr. James Aplan.

from the clothes lines. The snapping of the fresh laundry and the wives and children of the regiment stood waving small flags made from sticks and handkerchiefs, in the cool morning breeze, while tears streamed down their cheeks. The officers were allowed to break ranks and say their farewells to their families. Then, as suddenly, a sad stillness prevailed and enveloped the entire setting. General Terry and Custer wheeled their horses westward departing Fort Abraham Lincoln with a force of 12 companies of Seventh U.S. Cavalry 28 officers and 700 men; 3 ¹/² companies of Infantry (6th, 17th and 20th Infantry 10 officers and 167 men) three 1/2 inch Gatling guns drawn by four condemned cavalry mounts for each piece, handled by 2 officers and 32 men from the 20th Infantry. A drove of 110 cattle, 150 wagons (114 were six-mule government wagons) two hundred packers, teamsters, and herders and 45 Indian Scouts, guides and interpreters. A total of 52 officers (including four contract surgeons and one veterinary surgeon) 879 men and 1,694 animals.[79][125][131][132][133] Also along despite General Sherman's caveat, was Mark Kellogg reporter for the Bismarck Tribune.

"Nature gave us a send off this morning with a beautiful sunrise, followed by a heavy fog. A beautiful rainbow was formed in the fog, under which nearly the whole of the expedition passed." [134] When the band struck up "The Girl I Left Behind Me" the officers remounted their horses and rejoined their companies. And unlike the Black Hills Campaign, Mary Adams was allowed to accompany the column while Libbie and Margaret rode at the head of the command. When Libbie glanced back she saw a mirage. As if their forms were reflected from the opaque mist of the early dawn, the soldiers seemed as though they were riding into the heavens.[4]

Legend
By William Heyen

What did it signify, then, that as the 1200 men
of the 7th Cavalry Regiment set out
in a two-mile column from Fort Abraham Lincoln
in the mists of that early May morning,

they beheld a mirage; themselves in the sky,
there they were, wavery but clear where
some had before seen sylvan landscapes,
or lakes, or huge fish that once swam here?...

But now the soldiers themselves were caravan,
but bodiless, each man or horse or wagon in a kind
of trance. Even when Custer halted the column,
they all moved in apparitional undulation,

staying but going, undetermined, willful, in spelled
passage so beautiful, so biblical,
but more: as though they'd been here before,
as though they'd be here forever; but, no, as though

the column in all that vast language of sky
had only marked time, for them, for synchrony,
as though that legend awaited them,
already written, could, as it were, continue.[2]

Custer stood in his stirrups and glanced back at the undulating snake that was the Dakota Column.

All that he was, everything that he had become, his life up to this point was brought to bear.

As a small boy he'd read Fenimore Cooper, and he'd been taught the ways of the west by Cooper's grand nephew. He'd drilled with the New Rumley Invisibles and marched at West Point with the elite of the Army. He'd listened to the Veterans of the War of 1812 and became a veteran himself leading charges from Gettysburg to Appomattox. He rode with Buffalo Bill and the Brule in hunts on the prairie and hunted Cheyenne to the Lodge of the Medicine Arrow Keeper. He sat behind while his command rode off into the field and stood up for Indian Rights in Washington against a corrupt administration. Now he was back. The creaking of leather, the jingle of sabres, the chatter of the troops and the baying of the hounds assured him he was in

O. S. GOFF.   FORT LINCOLN, D. T

Private John Burkman "Old Nutriment".

'Valley of the Shadows'. By Michel Schreck.

Several days of continuous rains had all but brought the Expedition to a standstill. Upon reaching the border of Dakota and Montana a freak snow storm paralyzed the Column for several days in the beginning of June. Like his childhood hero, Natty Bumppo (the protagonist of James Fenimore Cooper's pentalogy of novels known as the Leatherstocking Tales) Custer spent a great deal of this time reconnoitering and hunting with his scouts away from the command despite Libbie's harsh admonitions that he not do so. Four of his favorite hunting hounds, Tuck, Lady, Swift and Kaiser were kept busy tracking and running down small game that supplemented the officers' mess and brought variety to their meager diets. His greyhounds were relying on their excellent sight to run down hare while the beagles, were constantly on the scent trail ducking in and out of coulees flushing out a cove of prairie hens or quail. *"Your correspondent had the pleasure of accompanying the scouting party,"* Wrote Mark Kellogg, *"Nothing daunted him (Custer) on he goes, never tiring, his boundless energy and will overcoming all seeming obstacles."* [3]

General Crook known to the Apache as "Nan Tan Lu Pan" the Gray Fox, with the cavalry-Infantry Wyoming Column of 800 men was finally able to leave Fort Fetterman on May 29. Later he would link up with Shoshone and Crow warriors boosting

steep perpendicular banks hemmed in by sporadic cottonwood, willow and sagebrush shoots. All the while the troops and animals were being savagely attacked by enormous clouds of mosquitoes.[79]

Because of the vast amount of country the campaign was to encounter, The Dakota Column was only part of the overall movement. The Seventh Cavalry divided itself into two wings; the right commanded by Major Reno and the left headed up by the senior Captain Frederick Benteen, would eventually cover over 400 miles in 39 days; with a total of 25 campsites for the entire campaign. Troops under the command of Generals Terry, Gibbon and Crook were to work in tandem. General Sheridan viewed it quite succinctly, *"General Terry will drive the Indians toward the Big Horn valley, and General Crook will drive them back toward Terry, Colonel Gibbon moving down on the north side of the Yellowstone to intercept...The result of the movements of the three columns may force many of the hostiles back to the agencies..."* [125] Hopes were of snaring the hostiles en mass and by now all signs pointed toward the vicinity of South Eastern Montana.

Major Marcus Reno.

'The Way to Valhalla'. By Michel Schreck.

his force to over 1,325 men.[82] Colonel Gibbon's force known as the Montana Column, consisted of five companies of the 7th Infantry and four companies of the 2nd Cavalry approximately 450 men departed from Fort Ellis in early April and had the task of patrolling the North Bank of the Yellowstone.[136] Already at high flow the river itself was a natural obstacle for preventing the hostiles escape into the Canadas. Numerous trails indicated a divergence into the Powder River Country; a flat arid powdery basin, pock marked by sagebrush, bunch grass and blooming yucca. Scraped, scarred, and rutted by arroyos, coulees and dry river beds all at once a part of an ancient sea that supported aquatic life imbedded in the gray and purple strata of the bordering bluffs and foot hills of the Big Horns. The crumbling feldspar, quartz, and marble refracted the light and cast shadows on sand, grass, and twisted rock. Along with the petrified wood that had once been a forest of an extinct species had since passed that dominion to the birds and insects commuting in their evolutionary march along the food chain. The dogs ranged out in fan shaped missions, each exploring and curiously disturbing rattle snake, prong horns and the occasional mule deer. All of this to the accompanying cacophony of grinding wheels, creaking leather, and metallic tones of a formidable city on the move. That they had gotten this far bore testament to an officer endowed with foresight, endurance, and passion for the chase.

On June 2, a telegram from Sheridan was sent to General John Pope indicating more Indians were now off the Reservation. Crook in the field had left a gap in the protection of the Wyoming-Nebraska border. Since more bucks had jumped the agencies,

Grant Marsh.
Captain of the Far West.

General George Crook.

a mass exodus would only encourage more to leave the reservations.[141]

That same day a telegram from Captain W. H. Jordan to Major E. F. Townsend read, *"...from my own knowledge I believe that at least 2000 Indians (1500 Sioux and 500 Cheyennes) men women and children have left the Agency here and gone north since the 10th ultimo, containing among the number at least 500 warriors..."* [143]

By mid-June a supply camp has been established at the mouth of the Powder River. Several Companies of the Infantry were assigned the task of guarding the depot while Grant Marsh and the "Far West" alternated with "The Josephine" continued to ferry supplies up the Yellowstone. Felix Vinitieri and his Seventh Cavalry Band became at this point dismounted and their white horses sequestered as remounts to be utilized for the rest of the campaign. This would be the first time the Seventh had given up their band and their sabres; and along with Custer's hunting hounds and the Supply Wagons, they would remain at the Powder River Camp for the duration. The mule teams began their conversion to pack animals. Each carrying approximately 250 pounds could travel five miles an hour up to about 25 miles a day.[137] On June 9, Reno had drawn his assignment and departed the Supply camp on a scout. In a quest for glory, he pushes beyond the limits of his initial scout, but his timidity does not take him far enough in discovering the Indians. Jeopardizing the stealth of the mission by exceeding his orders, he is within miles of Crook's column now engaged in a battle taking place in the Rosebud Valley.

'Indian War Party'. By Frederic Remington.

Outnumbered, out-flanked and out-horsed, Crook's debacle with the Indians on June 17th has taken him out of the picture with casualties of 10 dead and 21 wounded.[138] The other commands still unaware never received word of his defeat and plans continued as previously arranged. The Gray Fox retired to a leisure two week vacation of trout fishing until reinforcements arrived.[139]

General Terry and Custer's Seventh continued west arriving at the Tongue River on June 16. There the remains of a Lakota camp was discovered. When Custer walked into the abandoned camp he was shown what appeared to be the bones of a soldier, all about him clubs and sticks as though he'd been beaten to death. Armstrong stood absorbed in silence staring down at the corpse. All of his senses were coming into play. All signs pointed to more than the government's estimate of 800 to 1500 warriors off the reservations. Autie Reed ran up to his uncle and informed him that Isaiah Dorman had discovered an Indian Burial Scaffold painted alternately black and red indicating a great warrior. The burial shroud was roughly unwrapped and the desecrated remains thrown into the river. A short time later Dorman was seen on the bank with a fishing pole, allowing the Arikara Scouts to believe he had used the dead Indian for bait.[13] The rest of the crude shelters made from drift wood were utilized for the troopers' campfires. Along with several Burial Scaffolds the troops desecrated, disturbed and robbed for souvenirs.[140]

The trickling brook made for a relaxing afternoon as the command played cards and rolled dice on a game of chance. Some of the more superstitious troops made out wills and wrote letters home. All too soon they were on the move, their bandanas pulled tightly to their faces as the trail dust lined with alkaline permeated their nostrils along with the smells of horse and human sweat mixed with sagebrush and pine. The Seventh continued marching cross country on to the confluence of the Rosebud, while General Terry boarded the steamer "Far West" and met up with Gibbon's command in camp on the north bank of the Yellowstone further west. Boarding the riverboat with his chief of cavalry Major James Brisbin, John Gibbon comes down the Yellowstone to confer with Terry and Custer at the mouth of the Rosebud on June 21. On board the "Far West" steamer the meeting takes place between the officers discussing the strategy for the rest of the campaign. No one has heard from General Crook. On a map laid out in the main cabin Terry has marked out with push pins his overall plan. Custer and the Seventh will continue to push westward while Gibbon's column will close in from the north. General Terry will return with Gibbon and Brisbin to the camp on the Yellowstone and conduct the rest of the campaign from Gibbon's column. Custer will be on his own. Offered four companies of the 2nd Cavalry and the Gatling Guns Custer arbitrarily refused. But did welcome the addition of six crow scouts who knew

Harry "Autie" Reed.   *An Indian Burial Scaffold.*

the country the command would be marching over.

Knowing the hostile would use their hit and run tactics and always stay on the move, Custer believed the only way to defeat this enemy was to catch them napping. When offered the battery of Gatling Guns, he'd turned them down, claiming they would impede his march and thwart his element of surprise. The guns were mounted on fixed carriages, pulled by condemned cavalry mounts. Getting Indians to ride straight onto a rapid firing Gatling was a trick he'd not figured out, if he could even get the guns across the broken terrain he was sure to encounter. All were in agreement, Custer would make the first strike, he is to be the hammer to Terry-Gibbon's anvil.

Headquarters of the Department of Dakota
(In the Field)
Camp at Mouth of Rosebud River, Montana
Territory June 22ⁿᵈ, 1876

Lieutenant-Colonel Custer, 7ᵗʰ Calvary

Colonel: The Brigadier-General Commanding directs that, as soon as your regiment can be made ready for the march, you will proceed up

the Rosebud in pursuit of the Indians whose trail was discovered by Major Reno a few days since. It is impossible to give you any definite instructions in regard to this movement, and were it not impossible to do so the Department Commander places too much confidence in your zeal, energy, and ability to wish to impose upon you precise orders which might hamper your action when nearly in contact with the enemy. He will, however, indicate to you his own views of what your action should be, and he desires that you should conform to them unless you shall see sufficient reason for departing from them. He thinks that you should proceed up the Rosebud until you ascertain definitely the direction in which the trail above spoken of leads. Should it be found (as it appears almost certain that it will be found) to turn towards the Little Bighorn, he thinks that you should still proceed southward, perhaps as far as the headwaters of the Tongue, and then turn toward the Little Horn, feeling constantly, however, to your left, so as to preclude the escape of the Indians passing around your left flank.

The column of Colonel Gibbon is now in motion for the mouth of the Big Horn. As soon

'The Custer Brothers'. By Michel Schreck.

as it reaches that point will cross the Yellowstone and move up at least as far as the forks of the Big and Little Horns. Of course its future movements must be controlled by circumstances as they arise, but it is hoped that the Indians, if upon the Little Horn, may be so nearly inclosed by the two columns that their escape will be impossible. The Department Commander desires that on your way up the Rosebud you should thoroughly examine the upper part of Tullock's Creek, and that you should endeavor to send a scout through to Colonel Gibbon's command.

The supply-steamer will be pushed up the Big Horn as far as the forks of the river is found to be navigable for that distance, and the Department Commander, who will accompany the column of Colonel Gibbon, desires you to report to him there not later than the expiration of the time for which your troops are rationed, unless in the mean time you receive further orders.

Very respectfully, Your obedient servant,
E. W. Smith, Captain,
18ᵗʰ Infantry A. A. J. G.[144]

Captain Marsh was able to ferry Mitch Bouyer, the half breed interpreter and the six Crow: Hairy Moccasin, White Man Runs Him, Goes Ahead, Half Yellow Face, White Swan and Curley over to Custer's bivouac. Shaking hands with all of them, Armstrong very exuberantly exclaimed, *"We are glad to have you. We sent for you and you came right away. I am going to fight the Dakotas and the*

General Alfred Terry.

Cheyennes. I understand the Crow are good scouts. I have called you here not to fight, but to trace the enemy and tell me where they are; I do not want you to fight. You find the Indians and I will do the fighting. When we win the fight, everything belonging to the enemy you can take home, for my boys have no use for these things."

The Crow all nod their accession. They thought of Custer as a kind, brave, and thinking man. And immediately gave him the name Ika' Dieux' Daka', Son of the Morning Star.

Writing to Libbie later, Armstrong explained: *"I now have some Crow scouts with me, as they are familiar with the country. They are magnificent looking men, so much handsomer and more Indian-like than any we have ever seen, and so jolly and sportive; nothing of the gloomy, silent redman about them. They have formally given themselves to me, after the usual talk. In their speech, they said they had heard that I never abandoned a trail, that when my food gave out I ate mule. That was the kind of man they wanted to fight under; they were willing to eat mule too!"*

As the Crow went into camp with the Arikara, Armstrong could hear the faint staccato beats of the Arikara Tom-toms begin. He was drawn by the melancholy chants and the stomp of their moccasins on the ground; "Mother Earth." He came to their camp with his pipe (Cannupa), his buckskin jacket thrown carelessly over his shoulders and sat next to the campfire and listened and watched as the Arikara danced and wailed their death songs. It was in truth when he held the pipe and told them

The Far West.

White-Man-Runs-Him

Curly

Hairy
Moccasin

White
Swan

Mitch
Bouyer

Goes
Ahead

Crow Scouts with Custer.

"Custer never dies-Custer Live Forever."

When he returned to his tent he found General Terry waiting for him. Unsettled he had sought out Armstrong, "Custer, I don't know what to say for the last."

"Say whatever you want to say."

" Use your own judgment and do what you think best if you strike the trail. And whatever you do, Custer, hold onto your wounded." Mary Adams who had been tending to his last minute needs bid them both good evening retiring to her cabin on the boat. The next morning she stayed aboard the "Far West" steamer and returned to Fort Lincoln arriving on July 4.[145]

When the steamer left the next morning multiple packages, letters, and items including an article for The Galaxy of Custer's "War Memoirs;" also Kellogg's dispatch to the Bismarck Tribune were aboard, "We leave the Rosebud tomorrow, and by the time this reaches you we will have met and fought the red devils, with what results Terry writes: remains to be seen. I go with Custer and will be at the death." [3]

The "Far West" also carried Terry's telegram to General Sheridan , "No Indians have been met with as yet; but traces of a large and recent camp have been discovered twenty or thirty miles up the Rosebud. Gibbon's column will move this morning on the north side of the Yellowstone for the mouth of the Big Horn where it will be ferried across by the supply steamer and thence it will proceed to the mouth of the Little Horn and so on. Custer will go up the Rosebud tomorrow with his whole Regiment and thence to the head waters and thence down the Little Horn. I hope that one of the columns will find the Indians." [138] On the morning of the 22nd under overcast skies and a cold north wind, the Seventh reviewed before Terry,

Charlie Reynolds.

O. S. GOFF,   FORT LINCOLN, D.T.

Gibbon and Custer, whose staffs watched as they marched out of the bottoms to the tune of "GarryOwen" played by the assembled 21 Trumpeters of the Regiment, each playing a certain key. Gibbon offering his hand to Armstrong while goading, *"Now don't be greedy Custer. Save a few Indians for the rest of us."*

"No, I Won't!" With that Armstrong turned and put his Santa Anna spurs into Vic's flanks and rode away. Gibbon sat for a moment with his mouth agape and turned toward Terry, *"Now what exactly did he mean by that?"*

By the time this column had left the Rosebud they were on light marching orders and would not have even put up tents. They may have covered themselves with their half shelters to keep off the dew. Custer retained a fly and on the night of the 22nd an officer's call was made and the officers of the Seventh met at Custer's tent.[175] Pack mules carrying fifteen days rations of hard tack, bacon, sugar and extra salt and over 24,000 rounds of ammunition were turned over to Lieutenant Edward Mathey. Each company would be responsible for the proper packing of the mules, one non-commissioned officer and six men would be assigned from each troop. Requiring 84 soldiers and packers to keep them up with the column. Also an additional 50 rounds of .45-55 carbine ammunition would be distributed per man. Individually each trooper would have 100 rounds carbine and 24 rounds for his Colt Single Action .45 Revolver as well as 12 lbs. oats for his mount. Right and Left wings were now abolished. There would be no bugle calls from this time forward.[137] *"Pack extra salt, we may be living on horsemeat before this campaign is through."*

"I believe General Custer is going to be killed." When Wallace was asked why he believed that he responded, *"I have never heard Custer talk in that way before."* [140]

The next morning June 23, at 5:00 AM Custer mounted and started up the valley with his two color sergeants. John Vickory of Company F was carrying the Headquarters Flag, a yellow flag with a brown eagle. Custer's personal guidon was assigned to Robert Hughes of K Troop. This was the signal for the command to fall in and move out.

The cliffs and river seemed to close in on the column, almost as if a suffocating vortex lured and was literally pulling the command to their destiny. Covering a lot of ground through the valley they came across three large abandoned campsites of the hostiles. After marching 33 miles the command went into camp at 5:00 PM. The next morning

some of the scouts reported what looked to be smoke signals in the direction of Tullock's Creek. It was in that direction George Herendeen was to ride with his report to General Terry. Custer for the time being held off sending him. Numerous abandoned Indian campsites had been passed over containing strewn bones and indiscriminate pieces of buffalo hides. The grass being nipped down by large pony herds. Bleached buffalo skulls stuffed with sweet grass were found on the site where the Sioux Sundance had taken place. Carved into the Deer Medicine Rocks were images of figures with locust legs falling head first to the ground. The Crow said the images were carved by the spirits. It was here that Sitting Bull offered up 100 pieces of flesh cut from both his arms by Jumping Bull his adopted brother while he danced for more than eight hour before collapsing into a trance. In his vision he saw soldiers falling head first into camp. *"I give you these for they have no ears."* [79] Sand pictures on the ground showed soldiers with their heads pointing toward a Sioux camp. The Indians scout know that a battle is soon to take place. The Arikara scouts tell Custer if the Sioux are over taken they will fight like a buffalo bull and the soldiers will run like women.[79] While Armstrong walks amongst the Sundance Arbor a wind blows up causing his personal guidon to fall to the ground. Lieutenant Wallace takes special note that it fell to the rear. An omen of defeat. Herendeen approaches Custer, *"General here is where I leave you to go to the other command."* Custer's non- response is almost as if he is listening something on the wind. Even with his mind preoccupied he walks to a recent scalp hanging from a lodge pole. Taking a knee he begins conferring with the scouts in sign language. They tell him only one man could have led those soldiers whose scalp now hangs from the sundance lodge: Nan Tan Lu Pan. Even with Crook's force of a thousand men against them, the Hostiles prove stronger than anticipated. Custer is told by the scouts they believe Crook has been defeated.[146] *"Can you explain why no one has heard from him?"* Armstrong seems quite troubled. *"General the scouts know of a place up in the Chetish, the Wolf Mountains where they might observe the Indians' encampment. It's a well know place they've used on horse raids before."*

"Is it far?"

"Several hours good ride from here. But I'm sure they can make it. At least these Crow can."

Armstrong instructed Charley Reynolds to take Lieutenant Varnum, Bouyer, and at least ten Indian scouts forward to the place they call the Crow's Nest.

At eight o'clock on the evening of the 24th, after marching close to thirty miles, the command makes bivouac at the junction of the Rosebud and Thompson Creek. One of the enlisted men, William Taylor remembered, *"The trail was growing fresher every mile and the whole valley was scratched up by trailing lodge poles. Our interest grew as the trail freshened and there was much speculation in the ranks as to how soon we should overtake the apparently fleeing enemy."* [147] The question arose that this area of ground repeatedly scratched by travois and pony tracks either revealed a larger gathering of Indians than first anticipated or were they just successive summer camps? In either case they now indicated a larger concentration of Indians off the reservations than Washington first believed there would be.

"Custer was in the habit of selecting, when possible, a spot of great natural beauty." [147] To the right of the campsite high perpendicular cliffs while on the left wild rosebushes skirted the winding fresh water creek. *"Custer's Headquarters which consisted of a single "A" tent close up to the high bluff, facing the river, before the tent he sat for a long time alone, and apparently in deep thought. I was lying on my side a short distance away, facing him; was it my fancy, or the gathering twilight, that made me think he looked sad, an expression I had never seen on his face before."* [147]

After a brief supper the fires were ordered to be put out. As dusk enveloped the valley about 9:30 PM it was heard, *"General's compliments... wants to see all the officers at headquarters immediately."* [140] Picking their way over prone and sleeping bodies toward a single solitary candle they found the General, who

'Indians Watching as Custer Approaches'. By Frederic Remington.

A scene from Arts and Entertainment's "America's Golden Cavalier" finds the author with binoculars at the actual 1876 Crow's Nest. Courtesy of Mary Desson.

informed them they would be taking up an immediate night march. It was his intent to get as close to the Indians as possible. For now it looked as if the trail crossed over into the Little Big Horn Valley and it was Armstrong's plan to rest the command on this side of the divide, crossing on the evening of the 25, and engaging the enemy on the 26. Reassured by Terry that he and Gibbon would be in position by the 26. As the party broke up, some of the younger officers joined in a chorus of "Annie Laurie" almost in a sad tone before commencing with, "Little Footsteps Soft and Gentle," and "Good Bye at the Door," followed by the "Doxology" and ending on a more upbeat "For He's a Jolly Good Fellow."

By 11:00 PM the night march was initiated. Because of the thick dust and moonless night it was impossible to see any distance ahead. The only way the troops were able to stay on trail or keep up with the column was by the men in front hitting cups on their saddle pommels and those following, directing their horses toward that noise. Close to 2:00 AM most of the troops had found their way into the camp and were dropping from their horses indiscriminately to catch a few hours of sleep. Alkaline coffee was brewed, but proved to be so bitter it was unable to be drank. Swilling the grounds of java in their cups and putting the moist liquid to their parched lips was as close to becoming "coffee coolers" as they got.

Burkman eventually was able to locate where Custer was sleeping. "I seen Custer layin' in the brush a leetle ways off, his hat pulled over his eyes. I took him some hot coffee and hardtack. When I spoke to him he didn't answer. He was sound asleep. I woke him up though, and gave him the coffee, thinkin' he needed it, maybe, more'n sleep. The ways things turned out I was allus glad I did that".

"When he drunk it he handed me back the cup and smiled. 'Thanks, John,' he says to me, 'I'll tell Miss Libbie when we git back how well you've been takin' keer o' me." [135]

Around about dawn the column was preparing coffee a quarter mile from the base of the Crows Nest where the scouts had been up all night searching for signs of the village. Just at the break of dawn they had seen the smoke from the camp fires and sent

word to Custer to come forward. He rode part way up the bluff and was met by the scouts who told him to look for maggots on a buffalo robe. This would be the movement of over 20,000 head of horse on the bench land to the west of the village. By the time Custer looked through a battered telescope furnished by one of the scouts the morning haze had obscured the valley and he "Could see no sign of Indians," nor could he could see any ponies.

Bouyer exasperatedly blurted out, "If you don't find more Indians in that valley than you've ever seen in your life you can hang me!"

"Damn sight of good it'd do to hang you!" Custer disgustedly turns and starts down the mountain retrieving his horse and rides toward the column that has moved up since he left. Turning to Gerard, Custer exclaimed, "Now who in the mischief moved that command?" Tom Custer comes riding up to his brother, responds, "The orders were to march and we marched."

One of the Arikara scouts comes galloping up. "What's he trying to say?" Gerard responds, "Says we've been discovered by the hostiles." Seems Sergeant Curtis of F Troop upon discovery of some missing packs had gone back trail to retrieve a box of hardtack that had come loose and fallen off one of the pack mules during the night march; happened upon an Indian breaking into the box, "our presence had been discovered and further concealment was unnecessary;...we would move at once to attack the village." [148]

"Sound Officer's Call!"

It was the first trumpet call in days. While the troops saddle and prepare to move out, Armstrong, and several of the Ree scouts squatted in a circle having a "talk" after the Indian fashion. The general was serious and the scouts seemed disturbed and nervous. When Bloody Knife stood up abruptly

'They Fought Custer.' by Michael Schreck. Left to right: Crazy Horse, Two Moon, Crow King, Sitting Bull and Gall.

and said something Custer was brought out of his reverie and asked the interpreter in a brusque manner, *"What's that he said?" "He says we'll find enough Sioux to keep us fighting two or three days."*

"Well, I guess we'll just have to get through them in one." Half Yellow Face turned toward him making sign and gibbered in Arikara, *"Today we go home by a road we do not know."*

'1ˢᵗ Lt. Cooke'.
By C. Gómez.

Anticipating the hostiles would break camp and flee he immediately prepared his troops to march. *"The first troop ready will lead off."*

Benteen speaks up, *"H Troop is fit and ready."*

"Very good Colonel you shall take the advance." Armstrong said as he removed his buckskin jacket, tying it to the back of his saddle. Captain Frederick Benteen was to take Troops D, H, and K approximately 125 men, on a left oblique in hopes of cutting off any inevitable escape of the village to the south. This march on a 45 degree angle would allow he would be in supporting distance of the regiment at any given time and able to be used in the combined attack. Major Marcus Reno with three Companies A, G, and M around 140 troopers, was to proceed down Ash Creek parallel to Custer's main column of Troops C, E, F, I and L totaling 225 cavalrymen. Company B under Captain McDougall would bring up the pack train of ammunition now regulated to the rear of the column.

The five companies under Custer's command topped the bluff to discover a lone teepee containing the body of a warrior named She Bear, killed at the battle of the Rosebud. The Indian scouts immediately began counting coup on the body and put the teepee to the torch. While the column rode up the scouts were singing their victory songs and hovering about the burning lodge. *"Move to one side and let my soldiers pass you in the charge. If any man of you is not brave, I will take away his weapons and make a woman of him."* [13]

From a small knoll Gerard observes around forty Sioux bucks riding toward the river, *"There go your Injuns General running like the Devil!"*

Reno received orders to immediately pursue and attack. He is told he will be supported by the whole outfit. Armstrong turns to Cooke, *"Send a messenger back to Benteen to hurry up the packs. Should any of the packs come loose cut 'em and abandon them."*

"Ride to Destiny". By Marck Churms.

The mules have become more important than the supplies they carry. Custer is thinking they may be used as breast works later on.

From a high ridge using Lieutenant De Rudio's Swiss Binoculars Custer observes the largest gathering of Indians ever on the North American Continent. More Indians than ever had assembled in any one place on the western plains. Over 4,500 Sioux, Cheyenne and Arapahoe were gathered under the combined commands of Indian leaders Gall, Sitting Bull, Crazy Horse, Two Moons and Rain-in-the-Face. By now all his instincts and doubts about the credibility of the government reports were wind on the buffalo grass. He had his work cut out for him today. Quickly he started forming several options in his mind but all that was negated when he saw the dust cloud to the north. Glassing the horizon he knew what he had to do.

"A cry was raised that the white soldiers were coming," Remembered Gall, *"and orders were given for the village to move immediately."* [149]

In the village One Bull the adopted son of Sitting Bull began preparing for battle, *"Parley with them, if you can."* He is instructed by the Medicine Man. *"If they are willing, tell them I will talk peace with them."* [150] That large dust cloud moving north was

the non-combatants. Custer knows if he can capture them, the entire village will capitulate and surrender. The women and children might be on the run, but the most fierce hostiles ever to conglomerate in a unified force were not fleeing, but readying

Roy Anderson captures the confusion of Reno's rout from the valley.

'P.S. Bring Packs'. By Michael Schreck.

village. There is no talking after this. Gall's wives were brought down in the first volley, *"My two squaws and three children were killed there by the pale-faced warriors, and it made my heart bad. After that I killed all my enemies with the hatchet."* [149]

"As I neared the village, the Indians came out in great numbers, and I was soon convinced I had at least ten to one against me, and was forced on the defensive." [92] Reno now pulled the command back into the timber. After a time the Sioux begin to penetrate the defenses and as Major Reno mounts up Bloody Knife sitting on a horse next to him receives a shot to the head, causing brain, blood and bone chips to completely cover Reno who in a mass panic leads a "Charge" across the river to a better defense on the bluffs. Many of his troops unaware of the withdraw are trapped in the river bottoms and left to their own designs. Those who follow on horseback are chased by warriors who claim it is a buffalo route and they knock each soldier from their chargers as they would in a bison hunt.

Having seen the size of the village, Custer changes his strategy, from an all out attack to setting up a holding position with the entire Regiment until the arrival of Terry and Gibbon on the following day.

Messages are sent to each of the separated battalions while the Sioux successfully keep the two columns separated and continue chopping them up piece meal.

Custer sends Three messages first with Daniel Kanipe, to hurry the packs. Followed by Giovanni Martini Custer's personal orderly being sent back to Benteen to hurry the packs with a note drawn by the Regiment's Adjutant William W. Cooke, which reads *"Benteen, come on- big village- be quick- bring packs. P. S. Bring packs."*

Cooke also pens a message to General Terry and hands it off to one of the troopers, possibly Nathan Short, *"And after a brief conversation, the trooper rode away, heading north. This trooper rode a sorrel-roan horse..."* The message never delivered, without a doubt was intended for the hand of General Terry. [148]

Short's horse with full equipment and carbine is discovered a week later at the Rosebud. His remains are not uncovered for almost a century.

Did he get confused in his ride to Terry and wander into a small band of hostiles that did him in?

After unsuccessfully sending Smith and Yates to the river to relieve Reno's beleaguered troops, Custer recalls them to a high bluff where Headquarters is

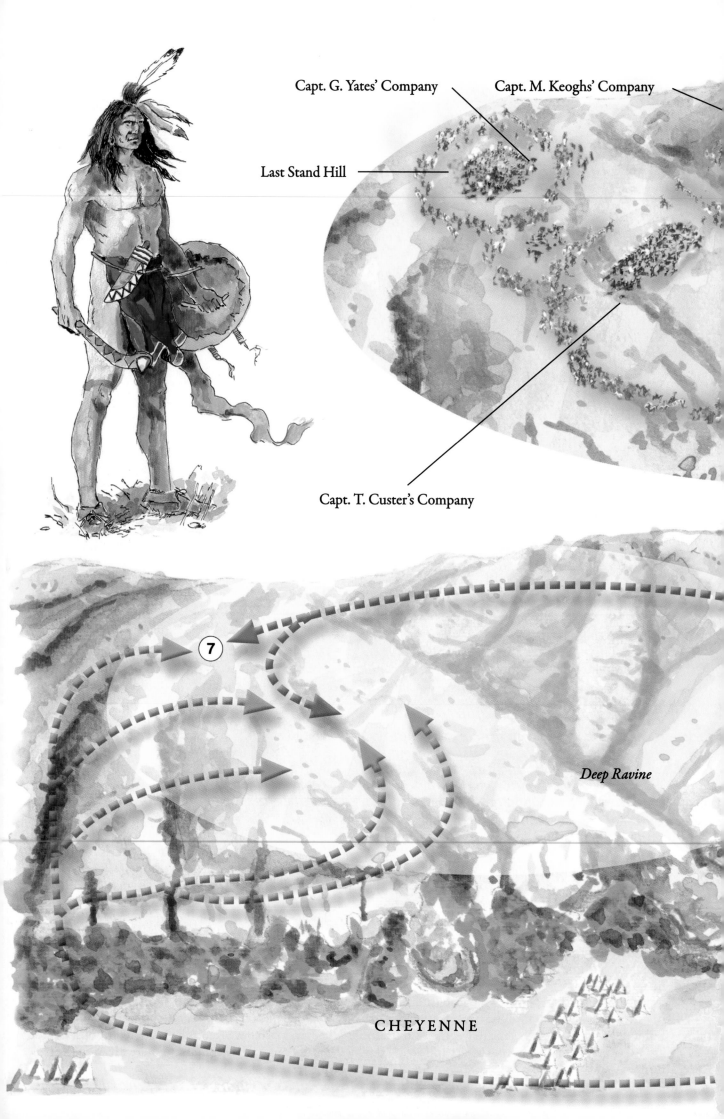

Capt. G. Yates' Company

Capt. M. Keoghs' Company

Last Stand Hill

Capt. T. Custer's Company

7

Deep Ravine

CHEYENNE

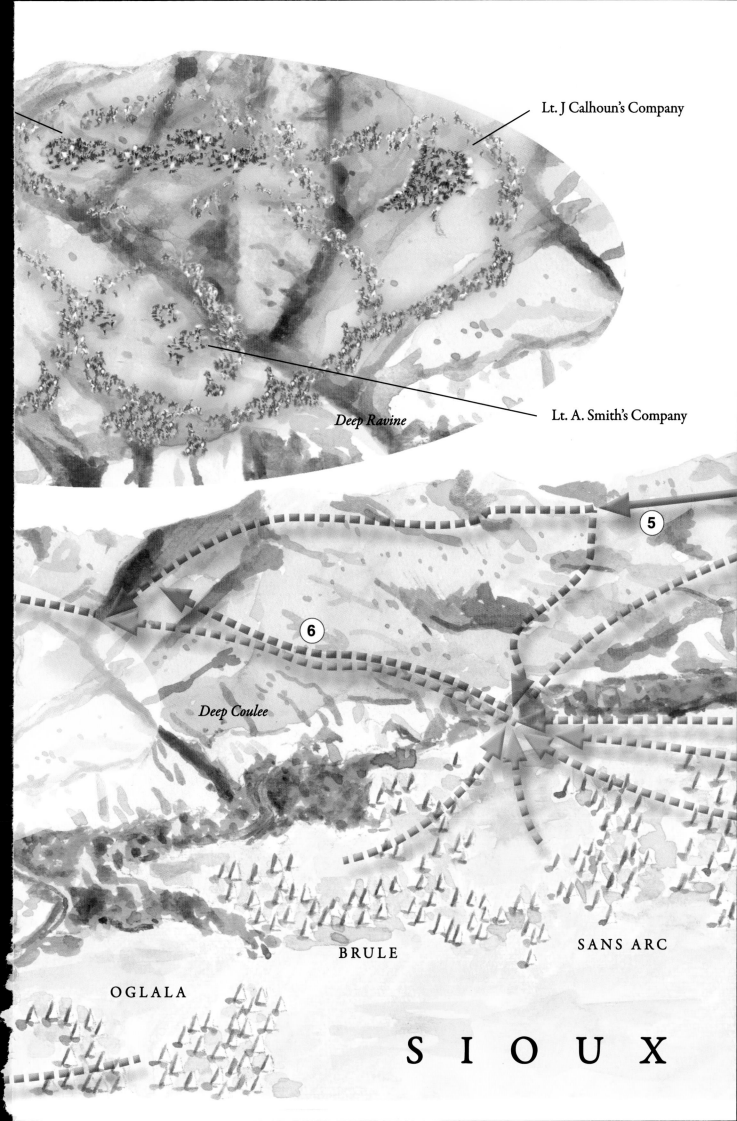

Lt. J Calhoun's Company

Deep Ravine

Lt. A. Smith's Company

5

6

Deep Coulee

OGLALA

BRULE

SANS ARC

SIOUX

to meet Custer or Reno's command now charging on the flat plain west of the Little Big Horn River.

Convinced Reno would catch the enemy napping Custer turns his field glasses toward the mounted force plunging forward in charge formation. Removing his hat Custer waves it in a rallying motion above his head. Or is it a recall "come to me" motion? Several of the mounts bolt forward beyond the column carrying uncontrollable horses and troopers into the enemies lines already coming out of the village to meet the attack. Dewey Beard having secured his war pony rode forward and observed, *"I saw a long column of soldiers coming and a large party of Hunkpapa warriors, led by Sitting Bull's nephew, One Bull, riding out to meet them. I could see One Bull's hand raised in the peace sign to show the soldiers that our leaders only wanted to talk them into going away and leaving us alone. But all at once the soldiers spread out for attack and began to fire, and the fight was on."* [150]

Quickly dispatching Trooper McIllhargy, Reno sends Custer the message, *"Enemy in front and very strong."* Awake and alert to his advance, they were able to force Reno into a haphazard retreat cutting him off from support and communication with Custer. *"I could not see Custer or any other support, and at the same time the very earth seemed to grow Indians, and they were running toward me in swarms, and from all directions."* Major Marcus Reno. *"I think we were fighting all the Sioux nation, and also all the desperadoes, renegades, half-breeds and squaw men between the Missouri and the Arkansas and east of the Rocky Mountains, and they must have numbered at least twenty-five hundred warriors..."* [151] Sitting Bull ran out of his lodge to inspire the warriors, *"Warriors, we have everything to fight for, and if we are defeated we shall have nothing to live for; therefore, let us fight like brave men."* [152] Reno dismounts the troops and a great barrage of gun fire is directed toward the

'Custer's Last Ride'. By Marck Churms.

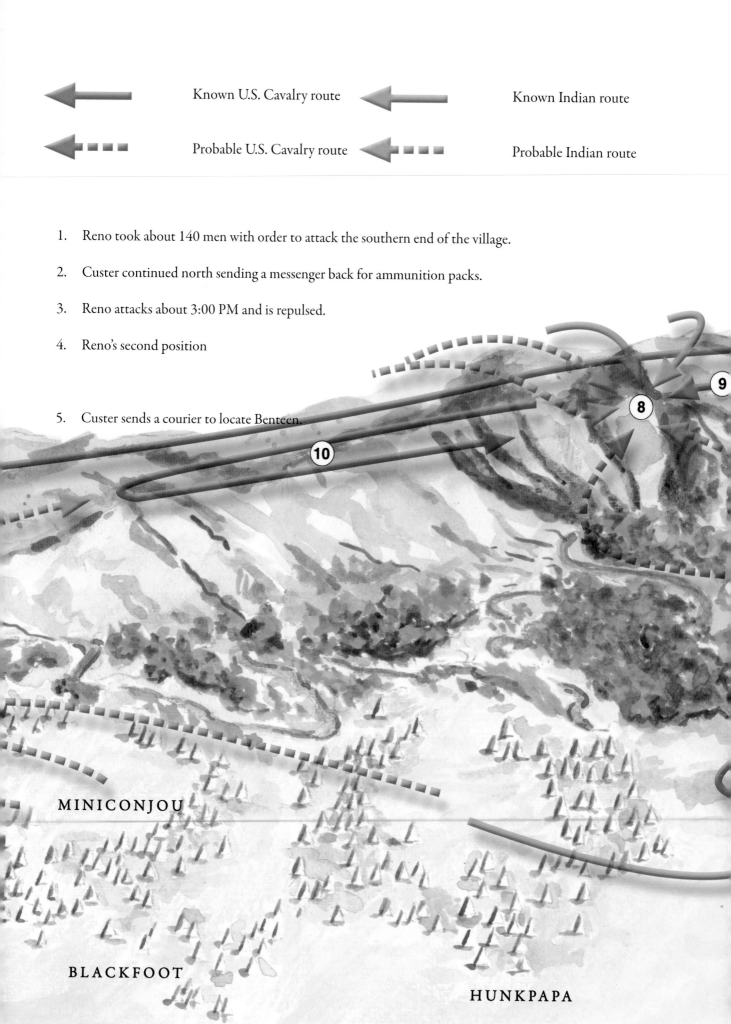

Known U.S. Cavalry route

Known Indian route

Probable U.S. Cavalry route

Probable Indian route

1. Reno took about 140 men with order to attack the southern end of the village.

2. Custer continued north sending a messenger back for ammunition packs.

3. Reno attacks about 3:00 PM and is repulsed.

4. Reno's second position

5. Custer sends a courier to locate Benteen.

MINICONJOU

BLACKFOOT

HUNKPAPA

6. Custer's battalion under attack by the Indians led by Gall.

7. Hand-to-hand combat at Last-Stand-Hill against the Oglala Sioux warriors led by Crazy Horse.

8. Custer and his men are killed and warriors attack on Reno's troops.

9. Benteen returns about 4:15 PM.

10. Warriors turned back Captain Thomas Weir attemp to join Custer's position.

Custer's last stand
June 25, 1876

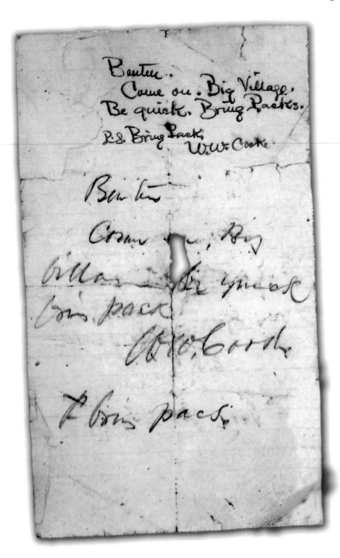

hope for the five surviving companies. Once the men were dismounted the warriors began waving blankets and blowing eagle bone whistles that frightened the horses and caused them to bolt, thus negating the soldiers' means of escape. Two Moon, War Chief of the Cheyenne said *"The shooting was quick: pop-pop-pop-very fast. Some of the soldiers were down their knees, some standing. The officers were all in front. The smoke was like a great cloud, and everywhere the Sioux went the dust rose like smoke. We circled all around them-swirling like water round a stone."* [152]

Instructing the men to shoot their horses for breast works it becomes *"Root Hog or Die"* for what remains of the five companies under Custer's command. Headquarters exists on a long back-bone of a high ridge running obliquely from the river. From this vantage point Armstrong can see down into the Indian camp, which stretches from three to five miles long. Its length is the distance between he and Reno defense to the south. As more and more braves join in the attack against Son of the Morning Star it becomes apparent this site may not be able to be held with so little of the command left. Thirty-nine horses are shot to protect between forty and fifty survivors of Custer's command. [148]

A signal fire is arranged with three distinct volleys. It is heard by Captain Weir who asks permission to ride to the sound of the guns. When permission is denied he mounts and rides north with most

forming up. There are a few casualties from Troop E and F when they withdraw. Lt. Harrington is shot midstream and his body washes away never to be found.

Mitch Bouyer turns to Curley, *"Curley, you are very young-you do not know much about fighting. I am going to advise you to leave us and if you can get away by detouring and keeping out of the way of the Sioux, do so, and go to the other soldiers and tell them that all are killed. That man (pointing at Custer) will stop at nothing. He is going to take us right into the village where there are many more warriors than we have. We have no chance at all...make your way back to Terry and tell him we are all killed."* [141]

Meanwhile Benteen's column in a lethargic effort to respond to Custer's order to *"Come quick and Bring Packs"* happens upon Reno's hasty retreat and is able to provide stability to Reno who is clearly in over his head, which now sports a bandana as his straw hat was left in the valley.

The dispensation and orderly fall of Calhoun's troops and Keogh's troops is testament to the Indians total veracity. Last Stand Hill is the final beacon of

Curley. Crow Scout.

of his troop in hot pursuit. **What Custer's last thoughts must have been at that point can only be conjecture.** Looking through his binoculars he could see horsemen on Weir Point. They were waving their guidons. Custer instructed the soldiers to signal back.

Sergeant James Butler, who had one of the last remaining horses on Last Stand Hill is called forward. It's known he has one of the fastest horses in the regiment. *"Can you make it to where those guidons are?"* Snaps Custer. *"I can surely try."* Would he be able to get through to Reno and have him join up with Custer's command?

Once he topped the ridge he was out of sight. Later Butler's body was found at the head of Medicine Tail Coulee a handful of cartridges all about his body. He had sold his life dearly.

All of this was observed by Captain Weir and his column from a high promotory between the two battlefields. Unaware of Benteen's approach as he gazes through his binoculars, Weir drops them when Benteen rides up. *"You've been recalled back."*

"But sir?" Answered an astonished Weir.

Benteen looked directly into his face and said, *"Everything you saw today, you men had better forget."* Reluctantly they begin their withdrawal back to Reno-Benteen Defensive Site.

Captain Thomas Weir.

'With Their Boots On'. By Michael Schreck.

'Custer Last Stand'. By Edgar Paxson.

Three miles away, arrows began raining down upon the troops who were trying to defend the last stand position. Some were having difficulty removing spent cartridges from their carbines. Verdigris that had formed on the copper casings from the curing leather caused them to stick in the breech and they had to be removed with jackknives. Custer's men were breaking blades and being shot before they could complete the process. Many were wounded having received hits by the smaller calibre Winchester and Henry Repeaters supplied to the Indians by the unscrupulous Indian Agents. Not clean kills; only wounds that knocked them down, later to be finished off by the Indian Women and children that would club them with stone mallets. The heavy blue-white smoke and sagebrush continued to conceal the Indians ever increasing numbers and movements toward the small knot of soldiers still remaining on Last Stand Ridge. By this time,

Boston, Autie Reed and the Reporter Kellogg had all gone under.

Riding to the front of the warriors Crazy Horse calls to them, *"Ho-ka Hey! It is a good day to fight! It is a good day to die! Strong hearts, brave hearts, to the front! Weak hearts and cowards to the rear."* [1] Lame Whiteman calls out, *"Come. We can kill all of them."* Wooden Leg explained, *"All around, the Indians began jumping up, running forward, dodging down, jumping up again, down again, all the time going toward the soldiers..."* [153] White Bull saw *"One soldier still alive toward the last wore a buckskin coat with fringes on it. I thought this man was leader of the soldiers, because he had ridden ahead of all the others as they came along the ridge. He saw me now and shot at me twice with his revolver, missing both times. I raised my rifle and fired at him; he went down. Then I saw another soldier crawl over to him..."* [150]

'Here Fell Custer', painted by Eric Von Schmidt in 1976, is Little Big Horn Battlefield National Monument official painting.

One of the Arapaho Warriors, Waterman said, *"...he was on his hands and knees. He had been shot through the side and there was blood coming from his mouth. He seemed to be watching Indians moving around him. Four soldiers were sitting up around him, but they were badly wounded. All the other soldiers were down. Then the Indians closed in around him..."* Tom rushed to his brother's side cradling him in his arms. He reached down to Armstrong's boot and pulled the .41 calibre Colt out putting it to Autie's left temple. The shrilling of eagle bone whistles and crashing of gunfire intermixed with the small pop of the discharged revolver. Lying his big brother gently to the ground he grabbed his rifle and pushed another shell into the chamber.

White Bull Sitting Bull's Nephew remembered, *"One soldier fired a rifle at me, then threw it at my head. He tried to wrestle with me. I had a bad time keeping him from getting my rifle. He began hitting me in the face. Then he grabbed my long hair in his hands and tried to bite my nose off! Two Lakotas came running up and began hitting the soldier with their war clubs. He let go of me. I knocked him down with the butt of my rifle."* [150] Tom was one of the last to go under. For him the reprisals were very bitter. Rain-in-the-Face came onto the scene and remembered the vow he had made two summers before. The battle lasted as long as it takes a hungry man to eat his meal.

Before the sun set on the Montana prairie, G. A. Custer had completed his journey To The Little Big Horn and Glory. On a hot June Sunday, at thirty six and a half years old he took his last breath. Few have embodied the courage and martial spirit of George Armstrong Custer. Fewer still who have attracted the scorn and wrath of political correctness aimed at the one single day of his life given up in the service of his country on the windswept plains of Montana. When Custer was defeated the War Department received the necessary funds to deal with the hostile Indian problem. Incarcerated on Reservations the nomadic people became a defeated people and wards of the government. For a man who had gone to Washington to defend them he became the scapegoat for those corrupt government policies he tried to expose. History would be altered by revisionists who needed Custer as the antithesis of the American Indian. For a time he was made a martyr for the nation shocked by the death of their Romantic Hero, the Boy General-George Armstrong Custer.

'His Brother Keeper: George and Tom Custer, 1876'. By Mark Churms.

On the evening of the 25th amidst the loud whoops and constant drumbeats men at Reno Hill could make out eerie shaped images before the large bonfires in the village. The screamers were undoubtedly captured troopers whose remains were found amongst the burned ashes in the village. Red Horse recalled that, *"The Sioux took the guns and cartridges off the dead soldiers and went to the hill on which the soldiers were, surrounded and fought them with the guns and cartridges of the dead soldiers not divided I think they would have killed many Sioux. The different soldiers that the Sioux killed made five brave*

stands. Once the Sioux charged right in the midst of the different soldiers and scattered them all, fighting among the soldiers hand to hand."

Yet Sitting Bull admonished, *"I warned my people not to touch the spoils of the battlefield, not to take the guns and horses from the dead soldiers. Many did not heed, and it will prove a curse to this nation. Indians who set their hearts upon the goods of the whiteman will be at his mercy and will starve at his hands."* [152]

'Custer's Last Fight'. By William R. Leigh.
Woolaroc Museum, Bartlesville, Oklahoma.

'Custer's Last Stand', General George Armstrong Custer at the Battle of Little Big Horn, 1876.

Remembering that victory Low Dog spoke very reverently, *"no whiteman or Indian ever fought as bravely as Custer and his men. The next day we fought Reno and his forces again, and killed many of them. Then the chiefs said these men had been punished enough, and that we ought to be merciful, and let them go."* [149]

Reno-Benteen Defense Site would view one of the most impressive scenes of the 19th Century, when the entire encampment on Pa Zees La Wak Pa moved across the valley like a giant carpet. Over fifteen thousand souls and 20 thousand horses left the valley burning the prairie in their wake.

Making his way across country, the young Crow Scout Curley manages to attract the sentries on the deck of the "Far West" that is moored at the confluence of the Big Horn and Little Big Horn Rivers. Once signaled aboard he begins rocking to and fro and lamenting the death of the Absaroke, the Crow Name for themselves, but this time applied to the soldiers in Custer's command. He drew in the dust on the top of a box two concentric circles, inside the circles he drew dots, *"Absaroke, Absaroke"* then made dots on the outside of the circles, *"Otoe Sioux, Otoe Sioux!"* Then in a swift gesture of his hand wiped the dots clean inside the circle. It immediately became apparent the message he was trying to convey to the men on the deck of the "Far West." [154]

Thomas W. Custer.

Skeptical, General Terry instructed Lt. Bradley to ride in the direction of the smoke cloud hanging over the Greasy Grass. At first they were convinced that Custer's Seventh had been victorious and was

'Red Victory'. By Michael Schreck.

Rain-in-the-Face.

hand appeared as though he had been holding something, possibly his RIC, that had been wrenched from it. He had a four inch knife gash to his thigh. The tip of his left little finger had been severed to remove his West Point Ring. And an arrow had been thrust into his genitals. [155]

Burkman helped in the recovery and burials, *"Custer is dead. The General is dead.. I was jist sorta numb all over and awful tired... I wished I could have gone along. I wish I could been thar at the last... Then all of a sudden it come to me that I wouldn't never agin hear the General laughin' and jokin'. Seemed like they want no use me goin' on."* [135]

That's when Tom Custer's body was found. He was lying face down, most of his scalp was gone but for a few tufts of hair at nape of his neck. Most of his skull had been crushed in with arrows shot into it and his back. His intestines were cut out and maybe his heart was gone. The only recognizable feature was the tattoo on his right forearm; The initials TWC with the goddess of liberty and the flag. He and Autie received the best burial, about 18 inches below the surface, since there were not enough implements in the command to do a proper burial.

Standing alone in Keogh's position was his horse Comanche, he'd had several wounds and was about to be destroyed when an objection was registered by Lieutenant Nowlan who cared and nursed the horse to the "Far West" where he was returned to Fort Lincoln and was forever after known as The Sole Survivor of Custer's Last Stand.

For Captain Grant Marsh he would be remembered as the "Last of the Argonauts" for his long standing Record Run of the Far West to Bismarck in 54 consecutive hours, covering some 710 river miles with Comanche and Reno's wounded from the Little Big Horn. [130]

burning the Indian Village and their stores. But all that changed when they approached and discovered the bodies on Last Stand Hill *"How white they look-Oh how white they look!"*

Benteen's exclamation upon looking down at Custer's corpse was as caustic as he was to Armstrong when he was alive, *"There he is God damn him. I guess he'll never fight again!"* Custer was on his back, his head uphill, his face skyward, his right heel against the body of a dead horse, his right leg across the body of a dead trooper who lay next to the horse. He was naked save for his white stockings. One of his wounds was a head shot in the left temple above the eye and had oozed blood down the left side of his face. The other a small calibre Winchester ball to the left breast. His right

Curly brings the news to the Far West.
By Charlie Russell.

7ᵗʰ Cavalry officers killed at the Little Bighorn

1ˢᵗ Lt. James Porter   1ˢᵗ Lt. Donald Mcintosh   1ˢᵗ Lt. James Calhoun   2ⁿᵈ Lt. Benjamin Hodgson

1ˢᵗ Lt. Algernon Smith   Lt. Col. G. A. Custer   1ˢᵗ Lt.William W. Cooke

Capt. George Yates   Capt. Thomas Custer   2ⁿᵈ Lt. Henry Harrington

Capt. Myles Keogh   2ⁿᵈ Lt. William Reily   2ⁿᵈ Lt. John Crittenden   2ⁿᵈ Lt. James G. Sturgis

'In the Arms of Immortality'. By Martin Pate.

Legacy of a Legend

"Captain, you are about to start on a trip with fifty-two wounded men on your boat. This is a bad river to navigate and accidents are liable to happen. I wish to ask of you that you use all the skill you possess, all the caution you can command, to make the journey safely. Captain, you have on board the most precious cargo a boat ever carried. Every soldier here who is suffering with wounds is a victim of a terrible blunder; a sad and terrible blunder." [156]

Immediately, even before the bodies of Custer's men were put into the ground, the finger pointing of blame began to take place. General Terry's instructions to Grant Marsh prefixed his reports to Generals Sherman and Sheridan. Scout Muggins Taylor rode west to deliver news to Bozeman which was transmitted to Helena where "The Independent" was credited with breaking the news of the Massacre.

Grant Marsh making his record run to Bismarck, arrived with derrick and jack-staff draped in black and the flag at half staff and made short work of off loading the wounded soldiers and Comanche at the Military Reservation. [157]

At 7:00 AM Captain William McCaskey, Lieutenant Charles Gurley and Doctor Johnson Middleton had the unpleasant duty of informing Libbie Custer of the tragedy. Sitting in the parlor on this hot July 6th morning she asked one of the domestics to bring her shawl as she had taken a chill. Then she rose to perform the task of informing the twenty-six unapprised widows at Fort Abraham Lincoln. [158] As they walked to the door Margret Calhoun who had been sitting quietly, apparently in shock, spoke up, *"Is there no news for me?"*

Indeed there was news for the entire Nation. J. M. Carnahan had been tapping a key continuously since the boat had docked, staying on the telegraph for over twenty-two hours informing the eastern press while Colonel Clement A. Lounsberry went to print with the Bismarck Tribune, *"Massacred General Custer and 261 Men the Victims. No Officer or Man of Five Companies Left to Tell the Tale..."*[157] No longer in the Army, Libbie Custer was about to face her biggest battle yet. *"I regard Custer's Massacre as a sacrifice of troops, brought upon by*

Libbie is informed of the tragedy. Illustration by E. L. Reedstorm.

Custer himself, that was wholly unnecessary-wholly unnecessary." [159]

Once the Democratic Press got hold of his comment Grant was forced to change his tune. Offering an olive branch, where once he'd held poison ivy, he made overtures for Libbie to come to the White House so he might comfort her or lend assistance. *"Mr. President, I would eat corn with the hogs before I would accept any help from you!"* [168] For the next 57 years Libbie would march on alone in her struggle to clear her husband's name. The first biography of the General published in December of 1876 by Fredrick Whittaker inspired an investigation into the causes of the Massacre and Letters to the press written by General Thomas Rosser, eventually brought about a Court of Inquiry into Major Reno's actions at the battle. Clearly a white wash of coached witnesses, Reno was cleared of all charges and exonerated.

Colonel Clement A. Lounsberry, who printed notice of the massacre with the Bismarck Tribune.

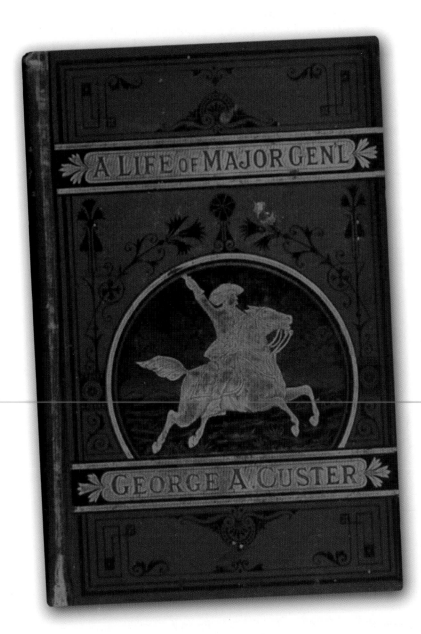

But for those gallant men of the Seventh who perished on the High Yellowstone, they would lie in shallow graves ravaged by time and predators. Indian Scout Dennis Moran claimed General Custer's bare and bleaching skull was partly sticking out of the ground.[161] This so upset the Country that a special detail headed up by Colonel Michael Sheridan and Major Joseph Tilford had the task of exhuming the remains and returning them to be properly buried at Military Cemeteries east of the frontier. During this mission David Reed was able to finance and retrieve the remains of his brother-in-law Boston and son Autie Reed to Woodland Cemetery in Monroe, Michigan. Tom Custer and James Calhoun were re-interned at Fort Leavenworth and Armstrong's corpse per his early request was brought to West Point.

"Popular Life of George A. Custer".
By his first biographer Frederick Whittaker 1876

A newspaper cut of the Reno Court of Inquiry held at Chicago in 1879.

"*On yesterday I shipped by U. S. Express via Chicago, the remains of your heroic husband General Custer to West Point, N. Y., care of the Commanding Officer of the Post.*" Major Tilford wrote Libbie. "*Those were my instructions from* General Sheridan. I presume an officer will accompany the remains from Chicago on.

It may be of some consolation for you to know that I personally superintended the transfer of the remains from the box in which they came from the

Custer was buried on the battlefield near the Little Big Horn, but in the following year his remains were removed and transferred back to the east. On October 10, 1877, he was given an elaborate funeral at the US Military Academy at West Point.

Libbie Custer and President William Howard Taft at the unveiling of the Custer's equestrian monument. Monroe, 1910.

battlefield to the casket which conveys them to West Point.

I enclose you a lock of hair from the remains which are so precious to you. I also kept a few hairs for myself as having been worn by a man who was my beau ideal of a soldier and honorable Gentleman."[162]

Besides the lock of hair from her husband, Libbie was given the battered commission case he had used on campaign to store his maps, one of the recovered Santa Anna spurs for which

James MacDonald's West Point depiction of G. A. Custer. August 30, 1879.

she returned to the Huger family and his favorite bowie knife she gave to his brother Nevin. The knife was used for many Thanksgivings to carve the bird. Nevin would ceremoniously exclaim, *"Feel honored that I am carving the turkey with the same knife General Custer scalped many an Indian with."* This guaranteed there would be plenty of left overs.

Even the small souvenirs could not mend a broken heart, *"A wounded thing must hide."* Libbie lamented that they had had no children.

Armstrong's remains were stored in a vault in Poughkeepsie, New York until fall when the Cadets returned to West Point. The Boy General's Coffin was then placed in state in the West Point Chapel; his dress helmet on the casket along with his Toledo Blade. On October 10, 1877 he was laid to rest escorted by The First Connecticut Cavalry who led the caisson sporting their Red Ties of the 3rd Cavalry Division.[162] Soon after School Children sent their pennies in order to erect a fitting monument that was placed to overlook the Hudson River. Libbie took umbrage to the foppish caricature and literally cried it off its pedestal. Although it was the first, it was not to be the last.

Custer statue in Monroe, Michigan.

Knowing of her disappointment in the West Point Statue, several groups began committees to come up with an acceptable monument and a proper location to have it placed. Armstrong's old command the Michigan Cavalry Brigade was leaning toward Lansing, Michigan the State's Capital. John Bulkley, Autie's old school mate and groomsman had proposed Monroe. Selection of a sculptor was equally challenging. After numerous candidates, Libbie was consulted and her preference went to Edward Potter. The price of his proposed equestrian monument was $25,000. Far more than the Monroe people could come up with. When the Brigade was approached for the joint venture, all that remained was naming the location? Libbie had always favored the home of her birth. After all when she and Autie spoke of "Home" it was always understood they meant Monroe. And so it was on June 4, 1910, with over 25,000 people and the

New Rumley, Ohio's 1932 Monument to G. A. Custer and his Great-grandnephew, Brice Custer "Setting the Record Straight" in his 1999 book "The Sacrificial Lion: George Armstrong Custer". Photo courtesy of John Hurless.

President of the United States William H. Taft watching, Libbie pulled the yellow ribbon revealing one of the most beautiful equestrian statues ever in her hometown of Monroe, Michigan.

One Hundred years later many would return to the town on the shores of Lake Erie to commemorate and remember.

In 1932 on the spot where he was born the State of Ohio placed their own version of the Boy General. It would be almost a century and a decade before another Custer would pick up the pen and slash away at the myths and untruths that surround the Legend and the Legacy. A military man himself, Major Brice C. Custer addressed a congregated group of "The Custer Memorial Association" at New Rumley, Ohio in front of the monument on June 4, 2005. The occasion marked his victory in getting the historical marker changed to represent the facts of his great grand uncle and not the popular tome that had been foisted for too many years at the site of his birth.

For the only woman to have ridden with the Army of the Potomac, Libbie had been forced to walk on alone. She lived a year following the battle at her home in Monroe before seeking employment in New York. The life insurance and small military pension was not enough to live on. She'd supplemented her life style with lectures, articles and books about her life with the Golden Cavalier.

To those who would besmirch her husband's name she stood up to them. Her three books: "Boots and Saddles;" "Tenting on the Plains;" and "Following the Guidon" became best sellers and she was in constant demand for the then popular traveling Chautauqua circuit.

Poets, Musicians and Artists portrayed their own interpretation of the event. From Walt Whitman's "Death Song for Custer"

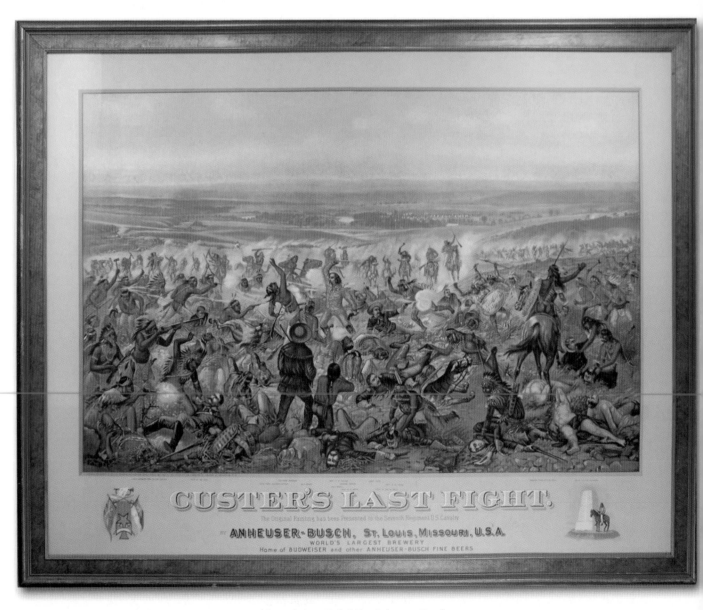

'Custer's Last Fight'. By Anheuser-Busch.

*2007 Recruiting Poster from IRAQ
featuring the author's image as G. A. Custer.*

"thou of the sunny, flowing hair, in battle,
I erewhile saw, with erect head, pressing ever
in front,
bearing a bright sword in thy hand,
Now ending well the splendid fever of thy
deeds,
(I bring no dirge for it or thee-I bring a glad,
triumphal sonnet;)
There in the far northwest, in struggle, charge,
and sabre-smite,
Desperate and glorious-aye, in defeat most desperate,
most glorious,
After thy many battles, in which, never yield-
ing up a gun
or a color,
Leaving behind thee a memory sweet to soldiers,
Thou yieldest up thyself.*[163]

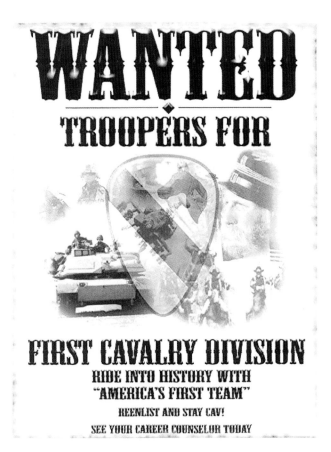

to the most popular Artwork known to man, the Anheuser- Busch painting: "Custer's Last Fight."

Sculptures abound portraying his victories and his defeat. His flamboyant ways have been the joy of artists who love the romance of the story and history and some just wanting to make a buck. In 1969 Don Russell complied "Custer's List" that verged on close to one thousand paintings alone; *"No single event in United States history, or perhaps world history, has been the subject of more bad art and erroneous story than Custer's Last Stand..."* [164]

Music would immortalize Armstrong for future generations with "General Custer's Last March;" the more recently resurrected compositions of Felix Vinitieri, set to CD by writer, composer and musician Steve Charpie; to Larry Verne's "Please Mr. Custer I don't want to go!"

General Custer's Image is an almost constant in news and literature having been used to sell products, display humor or even to recruit our modern military soldiers.

"If it makes better soldiers and men of them, why the necessity of knocking the paste eye out of their idol?" [165]

A DUEL WITH CHIEF YELLOW HAND.

*Engraving for the cover of the book 'First Scalp for Custer: The Skirmish at Warbonnet Creek'.
Nebraska, July 17, 1876, by Paul L. Hedren.*

Posters of Buffalo Bill's show and the famous Raoul Walsh's film.

As the tides changed Custer became even more a victim than the Indians who were the victims he defended. Wrapping it all in a nice package, failure of the Indian Campaign was blamed on Custer. *"It takes Courage to Kick a Dead Lion."* [14]

But there were still those who believed in and admired the Boy General. Buffalo Bill who had left the Theatrical Stage to go west upon learning of his friend's death was still wearing his stage cos-

tume when he slew Yellow Hand, a Cheyenne Chief at the Battle of War Bonnet Creek and pronounced, "The First Scalp for Custer!" [160]

The Wild West became the forerunner of Western Films and portrayals on the big screen from the silents to modern day there have been a list of films portraying G. A. Custer to the Little Big Horn. None stand out like Errol Flynn's portrayal in "They Died With Their Boots On." To a

Death of Custer - A dramatic portrayal of Sitting Bull stabbing Custer,
with dead Native Americans lying on ground, in scene by Pawnee Bill's Wild West Show performers. c.1905.

Richard Mulligan as the maniacal General G.A. Custer. 1970.

DUSTIN HOFFMAN
"LITTLE BIG MAN"
A Cinema Center Films Presentation

MARTIN BALSAM · JEFF COREY · CHIEF DAN GEORGE
Screenplay by Calder Willingham
Based on the Novel by Thomas Berger   FAYE DUNAWAY
AS MRS. PENDRAKE
A National General Pictures Release
Panavision® Technicolor® GP

Produced by Stuart Millar · Directed by Arthur Penn

Arthur Penn's irreverent view of Custer was evident in his film 'Little Big Man'. 1970.

newer generation they identify with, "Little Big Man" starring Dustin Hoffman in the title role and Richard Mulligan as a half crazed Indian Hating Custer. But history is oftentimes viewed through a warped prism. The Custer and Indian Wars history lives today as though its memory permeates our lives. Was it the significance of the man or that moment in history? Today for those who look they need go no further than the local museum, art galleries, movie rentals, online articles and book store.

Custer's legacy lives in annual works of research produced and re-produced in the long debate within The Little Big Horn Associates, Custer

Sioux veterans of the Battle of Little Big Horn on the battleground. c. 1927.

The Author and Ernie La Pointe, Great Grandson of Sitting Bull in front of Custer Monument. Monroe, Michigan.

Battlefield Historical and Museum Association, and the far reaching Custer Association of Great Brittan. All of whom make long sabbaticals to the National Monument; The Custer Battlefield Museum and Elizabeth Custer Library and Museum of Frontier Women of The West. They buy numerous published works visit gift shops and watch the reenactments. And like the Bermuda Triangle and Disappearance of Amelia Earhart, all profess to know the answer of what happened at the Little Big Horn in June of 1876.

The tales of Custer's Last Stand have varied from the day of the discovery of those still bodies found on the Montana Hill. Native American descendents of the Battle at Little Big Horn state the true story has been hidden by the whites for well over a 100 years while the Native version has been discounted and disregarded. It is said that as the only survivors of this great battle their oral history has been ignored as the Soldiers history and role in it

has been glorified. Fear shortly after the battle sealed the lips of those survivors and sequestered away the items taken from the field to avoid the whiteman's wrath. Only time and the desire to dispute the misconceptions of that day and the image of their forefathers has prompted the Native Americans in the later 20th and early 21st Centuries to come forward. Artifacts both found on the battlefield and sold by the tribes continue to tell the story which may never be fully known as the witness of the participants has long been silenced.

The Little Big Horn Battlefield today.

And what of the Lakota People? After the battle in 1876 many crossed the border to Canada and lived in peace until the buffalo became almost extinct. Forced to return to the land where he was born, *"The chiefs of old are gone."* Sitting Bull led his band into Fort Buford, *"I wish it to be remembered, that I was the last man of my tribe to surrender my rifle...* [166] *There are no Indians left but me!"* [167]

Killed by Indian Police just before the Massacre at Wounded Knee in December of 1890, his descendants carried the cannupa and the spirit on even venturing to Monroe, Michigan known as the Home of General Custer. *"I was invited to Monroe, Michigan in 2006."* said Ernie La Pointe the only living Great-Grandson of Tatanka Iyotake. *"I accepted the invitation because I believe in this motto 'Peace through Unity.'* He and the author have actively participated in Memorial Services each year at the battlefield and have given programs and lectures across the United States and Canada. Ernie has traveled to Europe and parts of Scandinavia promoting this message of peace. *"There have been many different books and movies made about this battle. The American historians and book authors have ignored the oral stories..."*

As a small boy he sat on his living room floor and listened to old warriors who had fought in the battle tell their stories in native tongue and sign language. And although no matter where he goes and is well received the questions always come back to *"Peji Sla Okiciza"* the Little Big Horn. *"I feel it is time to look toward the future, see how we as human beings can put our minds together, and see what kind of a world we can create for our future generations."*

Custer once wrote, *"...I desired to link my name with acts and men... not only for the present but for future generations."*

Libbie herself looked forward to a day, *"When tradition and history will be so mingled that no one will be able to separate them."* [47]

She survived her beloved Autie dying just four days shy of her ninety first Birthday in 1933. She lies next to the Boy General in a modest grave at West Point Military Academy.

It would seem the gunfire and war whoops almost a century and a half ago will reverberate like a stone thrown into a placid pond and the Legacy of a Legend will continue to be celebrated from Motion Pictures to Military Miniatures. *"Custer Never Dies-Custer Live Forever."*

Libbie Custer.

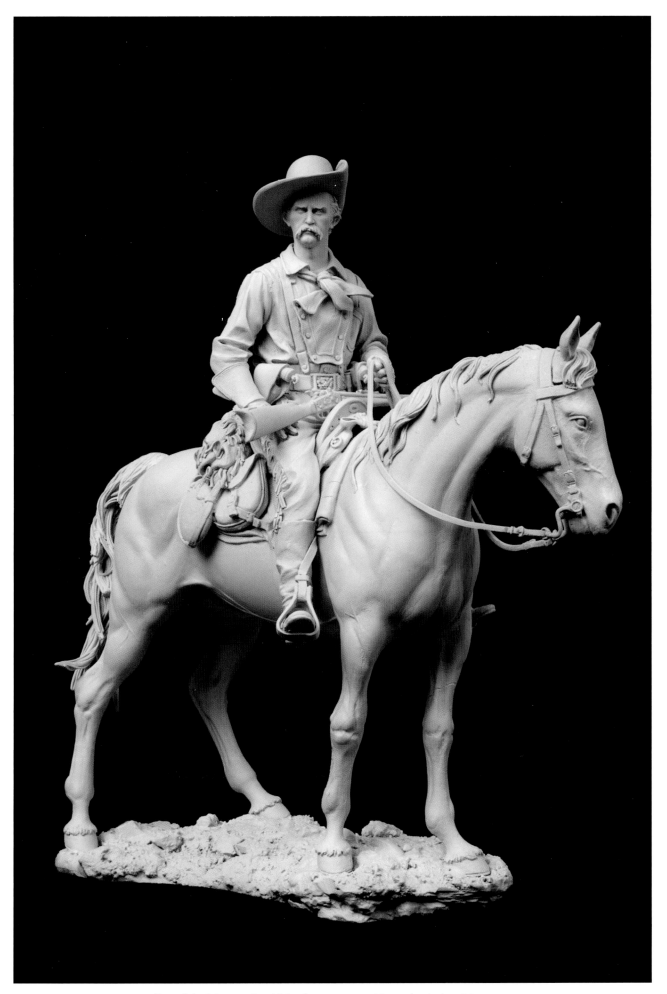

'Son of the Morning Star'. Metal miniature in 90 mm by Andrea Miniatures.

FOOTNOTES, BIBLIOGRAPHIES AND SOURCES

1. *Crazy Horse and Custer,* Stephen Ambrose. Doubleday and Co., Garden City, NY, 1975

2. *An Officer's Story & Legend, Crazy Horse in Stillness,* William Heyen. BOA Editions, Ltd., Brockport, NY, 1996

3. *I Go With Custer,* Sandy Barnard. The Bismarck Tribune, Bismarck, ND, 1996

4. *Boots and Saddles,* Elizabeth B. Custer. University of Oklahoma Press, Norman, OK, 1980

5. *A Summer on the Plains with Custer's 7ᵗʰ Cavalry: the 1870 Diary of Annie Gibson Roberts,* edited by Brian C. Pohanka. Schroeder Publications, Lynchburg, VA, 2004

6. *Following the Guidon,* Elizabeth B. Custer. University of Oklahoma Press, Norman, OK, 1966

7. *Custer and His Dogs,* James L. Pope. Phoenix Proprietary Publications, Plover, WI, 1990

8. *Nomad, George A. Custer in 'Turf and Farm.'* Brian Dippie. University of Texas Press, Austin, TX, 1980

9. *Custer, The Last of the Cavaliers,* Frazier Hunt. Cosmopolitan Book Corporation, NY, 1928

10. *The Redman, Cadet G. A. Custer* for Lt. Childs, Instructor of Ethics. May 5, 1858

11. *Sheridan: the Life and Wars of General Phil Sheridan,* Roy Morris, Jr. Vintage Civil War Library, NY, 1992

12. *The Reluctant Conquerors,* Thomas Leonard. American Heritage, Vol. XXVII, August 1976

13. *Arikara Narrative of Custer's Campaign and the Battle of the Little Bighorn,* Orin Libby. University of Oklahoma Press, Norman, OK, 1998

14. *Kick the Dead Lion,* Charles G. Du Bois. The Reporter Printing and Supply Co., Billings, MT, 1961

15. *The Custer Story,* Marguerite Merrington. The Devin-Adair Company, NY, 1950

16. *He Thought His Ancestors Came From Orkney,* Peter G. Russell. Western Publications, United Kingdom, 2001

17. *Custer Genealogies,* Milo Custer. Guidon Press, Bryan, TX (originally published in 1944)

18. *German Element in the United States: With special Reference to its Political, Moral, Social and Educational Influence,* Albert Bernhardt B. Faust. Houghton Mifflin Co., Boston, 1909

19. *The Descendants of Paulus and Gertrude Kusters of Kaldenkirchen, Germany and Germantown,* Pennsylvania: the first four generations, Jean White Castor. Association of America, Richmond, TX, 1991

20. *Custer Memorial Association Presents Swing Around the Circle,* E. Leroy Van Horne. Carrollton, Ohio, June, 2002

21. *General Custer and New Rumley,* Ohio, John M. Carroll. Bryan, TX, July, 1978 (reprinted by permission of Arrow and Trooper Publishing, Brooklyn and New York, April, 2001

22. Elizabeth B. Custer Collection, CBNM microfilm rolls 1-6

23. *Custer's Ohio Boyhood,* Charles B. Wallace. Harrison County Historical Society, Cadiz, Ohio, 1987

24. *Complete Life of Gen. George A Custer,* Frederick Whittaker. Sheldon & Co., NY, 1876

25. *The Boy General,* Bill Bailoff. Bend in the River (Magazine of the Historic Maumee Valley), July, 1986

26. *Traces of General George Armstrong Custer,* Ralph Naveaux. Monroe County Historical Museum, Monroe, MI, 2009

27. From conversations with 91-year-old George Schultz. History of New Rumley. Collected when E. Leroy Van Horne was a boy

28. *Custer Legends,* Dr. Lawrence A. Frost. Bowling Green University Poplar Press, 1981

29. *Witnesses for the Defense of General George Armstrong Custer,* W. Donald Horn. Horn Publications, Short Hills, NJ, 1981

30. *War Memoirs,* G. A. Custer. Galaxy Magazine, July, 1876

31. *Touched by Fire, The Life, Death, and Mythic Afterlife of GAC,* Louise Barnett, Henry Holt, 1996

32. *Spirit of Old West Point,* Morris Schaff. Houghton, Mifflin and Co., Boston and New York, 1907

33. *Bugles, Banners and War Bonnets,* Ernest L. Reedstrom. Bonanza Books, New York, 1986

34. *Letters from George, and Life of Gen. George Armstrong Custer,* L. Milton Ronsheim. The Harrisonian: Journal of the Harrison County Ohio Historical Society, Number 2, 1989:

35. *The 4th Michigan Infantry at the Battle of New Bridge, Virginia,* Martin Nino Bertera. Tillieagnes Press, Wyandotte, MI, 2003

36. *Portrait of a General,* W. Donald Horn. Southeast Publications, West Orange, NJ, 1998

37. *I, Elizabeth,* Ruth Painter Randall. Little-Brown and Company, 1966

38. *The Civil War Memories of Elizabeth B Custer,* Arlene Reynolds. University of Texas Press, 1994

39. *Custer Victorious,* Gregory Urwin. Associated University Presses, Inc., 1983

40. Equestrian statue of George Armstrong Custer; unveiling ceremonies at Monroe, Michigan, June 4, 1910

41. *East of Gettysburg,* David Riggs. Old Army Press, Ft. Collins, CO, 1970

42. *The Unforgettable Custers,* Stephanie C. Schuster. Real West, September, 1975

43. *Custer, The Controversial Life of G A Custer,* Jeffery Wert. Simon & Schuster, 1996

44. *Favor the Bold,* D. A. Kinsley. Holt-Rinehart & Winston, 1967

45. *Marriage of General Custer,* Monroe Commercial, February 11, 1864

46. *Mrs. Custer to Be Buried at West Point,* F. W. LaRouche. Monroe Evening News, April 5, 1933

47. *Elizabeth B Custer and the Making of a Myth,* Shirley Leckie. University of Oklahoma Press, 1993

48. *General Custer's Libbie,* Dr. Lawrence A. Frost. Superior Publishing Company, 1976

49. *Brighten the Corner,* Music History Committee and Fine Arts Council. Monroe Library, 1977

50. *The Custers in Monroe,* Thomas and Alice O'Neil. Monroe County Library System, 1991

51. *Custer: The Life of General G A Custer,* Jay Monaghan. University of Nebraska Press, Lincoln, Nebraska, 1959

52. *General Custer's Bride Was Glamorous,* Monroe Evening News, April 12, 1962

53. *The Victorian Wedding,* Parts I & II, M. Hoppe. Internet Online, 1997

54. *Marriage of Gen. Custer,* The Detroit Advertisor and Tribune, February 10, 1864

55. *Bride of Glory,* Margaret Leighton. Ariel Books, NY, 1962

56. *I Do, Said Gen. Custer,* The Billings Gazette, May 27, 1961

57. *Custer's First Last Stand,* John Barratt. Military Illustrated, Number 181, 2003

58. *Fightin' Tom Rosser, C. S. A.,* Millard and Dean Bushong. Beidel Printing House, Inc., Shippensburg, PA, 1983

59. From a tombstone at Hillcrest Cemetery in Jackson, Michigan. Corrupted from General Montgomery Meigs' formal entrance at Arlington National Cemetery. *Field Guide Fame's Eternal Camping Ground,* Kim O'Connell. Civil War Times Vol. XLIX No. 3, June, 2010

60. *Mexican Minister Describes Andrew Johnson's 'Swing Around the Circle,'* Thomas Schoonover. Civil War History, Vol. XIX No. 11, June 1973

61. *The View From Officers' Row,* Sherry L. Smith. University of Arizona Press, Tucson, AZ, 1990

62. *Custer for President,* Craig Repass. Old Army Press, Fort Collins, CO, 1985

63. *The Court-Martial of General George Armstrong Custer,* Dr. Lawrence A. Frost. University of Oklahoma Press, 1979

64. *Keep the Last Bullet for Yourself,* Thomas Marquis. Reference Publications, Inc., 1984

65. *Following the Custer Trail,* Laudie Chrone. Printing Plus, Bismarck, ND, 1997

66. *Battle of the Little Big Horn - History in Paint,* Alton Sissell. News Caster, Volume XXV Issue 3, September, 2007

67. *Curse Not His Curls,* Robert Ege. Old Army Press, Fort Collins, CO, 1974

68. *The Dress Uniform of the 7ᵗʰ Cavalry, 1872-82,* John Langellier. Military Illustrated Past and Present, No, 19, June/July 1989

69. *I Fought with Custer,* Frazier and Robert Hunt. University of Nebraska Press, Lincoln, NE, 1987

70. *Such Signal Success?* A collection of essays compiled and edited by Kevin Galvin. Volume 3 in the British Custeriana Series, Western Publications Limited, London, 2003

71. *Custer and the Cheyenne,* Louis Kraft. Upton and Sons Publishers, El Segundo, CA, 1995

72. *Of Garryowen in Glory,* Lt. Col. Melbourne C. Chandler. 1960

73. *My Life On The Plains,* G. A. Custer. The Galaxy, Vol. VII, January 1872 to June 1872

74. *Daily Life in a Plains Indian Village 1868,* Michael Bad Hand. Terry Clarion Books, 1999

75. *Trail of Tears,* Elliott West. Western National Parks Association, Korea, 2000

76. *Wild Life on the Plains and the Horrors of Indian Warfare,* General G. A. Custer. Sun Publishing Co., St. Louis, MO, 1883

77. *500 Nations,* Alvin Josephy. Gramercy Books, NY, 1994

78. *Bury My Heart at Wounded Knee,* Dee Brown. Holt, Rinehart & Winston, NY, 1970

79. *Custer's Luck,* Edgar Stewart. University of Oklahoma Press, Norman, OK, 1883

80. *Native American Indians: Quotes and Thoughts,* Steven Redhead. www.stevenredhead.com/Native/contact.html

81. *Frontier Soldier : An Enlisted Man's Journal of the Sioux and Nez Perce Campaigns, 1877,* by Private William Zimmer, edited by Jerome Green. Montana Historical Society Press, Helena, MT, 1998

82. *The Little Bighorn Campaign,* Wayne M. Sarf. Combined Books, Conshohocken, PA, 1993

83. *Indians and the Old West,* Anne Terry White. Golden Press, New York, 1958

84. *Book of Jeremiah (50:42),* King James Bible/Old Testament

85. *The Custer Tragedy,* Fred Dustin. Upton & Sons, El Segundo, CA, 1987

86. *My Native Land,* James Cox. Blair Publishing Co., Philadelphia, 1903

87. *Chiefs and Generals,* Richard Etulain and Glenda Riley. Fulcrum Publishing, Golden, CO, 2004

88. *The Tomahawk and the Flame,* Hans Von Stockhausen. www.angelfire.com/games3/jacksongamer/tomahawk.htm

89. *Indian Signals and Sign Language,* George Fronval and Daniel Dubois. Bonanza Books, New York, 1985

90. *The Plains Indians,* Jay Smith. Research Review: The Journal of the Little Big Horn Associates, Vol. 1 No. 2, December, 1987

91. *The Horsemen of the Plains,* Joseph Altsheler. The Macmillan Co., NY, 1966

92. *Little Big Horn 1876,* Robert Nightengale. Far West Publishing Edina, MN, 1996

93. *The Indian and the White Man,* Helen Hunt Jackson. A Century of Dishonor, Boston, 1887

94. *Buffalo Bill and the Wild West,* Henry Sell and Victor Weybright. The International Cody Family Association, Kissimmee, FL, 1955

95. *The Indian Dilemma-Civilization or Extinction,* Carl Schurz. *Annals of America,* Volume 10, 1866-1883. Reconstruction and Industrialization, Encyclopedia Britannica, 1976

96. *Campaigning In Kansas With Maida And Blucher, General Custer's Staghounds,* Don Schwarck. *Research Review,* The Journal of the Little Big Horn Associates, Vol. 6, No. 2, June, 1992

97. The Custer Album, Dr. Lawrence A. Frost. Superior Publishing Co., Seattle, 1964

98. *The Grand Duke Alexis in the United States of America,* William W. Tucker. Interland Publishing Inc., NY, 1972

99. *The Duke Alexis Hunt,* Medicine Creek Journals

100. *The Imperial Buffalo Hunt,* James Callaghan. Old West, Winter 1997

101. *Buffalo Bill: Last of the Great Scouts,* Helen Cody Wetmore. University of Nebraska Press, Lincoln, 1965

102. *The Lives and Legends of Buffalo Bill,* Don Russell. University of Oklahoma Press, Norman, OK, 1960

103. *The Smith and Wesson .44 Russian,* Donald Brown. Frontier Times, August-September 1963

104. *Russian Duke Hunted in Hayes County,* McCook Daily Gazette. Nebraska Centennial Edition, 1867-1967

105. *Custer, Cody and The Grand Duke Alexis,* Elizabeth B. Custer and John Manion. Research Review: *The Journal of the Little Big Horn Associates,* Vol. 4, No. 1, January, 1990

106. Quote by T. H. Watkins from the PBS series *The West,* as written in *Iron Horse and the Buffalo: Conflict on the Plains,* William Friedheim. (Internet)

107. *Transcontinental Railroad;* the film and more, from an Internet interview with Donald Fixico for American Experience.

108. *Jay Cooke's Gamble, The Northern Pacific Railroad, The Sioux and the Panic of 1873.* M. John Lubetkin University of Oklahoma Press, Norman OK 2006

109. *Custer's Seventh Cavalry Comes to Dakota,* Roger Darling. Upton and Sons, El Segundo, CA, 1989

110. *The Little Shadow Catcher = Icastinyanka Cikala Hanzi: D. F. Barry celebrated photographer of famous Indians,* Thomas M. Heski. Superior Publishing Co., Seattle, WA, 1978

111. *History of Fort Rice North Dakota,* Mrs. Anton Gartner. Bismarck Tribune, Centennial Publication of the Fort, 1964

112. *Arrest General Custer,* Dr. Lawrence A. Frost. Garry Owen Publishers, Monroe, MI, 1987

113. *General Custer and his Sporting Rifles,* C. Vance Haynes, Jr. Westernlore Press, Tucson, AZ, 1995

114. *Battling with Sioux on the Yellowstone,* G. A. Custer. The Galaxy July, 1876

115. *Exploring With Custer,* Ernest Grafe and Paul Horsted. Golden Valley Press, Custer, SD, 2002

116. *The 1874 Custer Expedition to the Black Hills,* South Dakota Visitor magazine, Spring, 2010

117. *Custer confirmed rumors, Black Hills Deadwood magazine,* July/August 1996. Vol. 6, No. 3.

118. *Custer's Prelude to Glory,* Herbert Krause and Gary Olson. Brevet Press, Sioux Falls, SD, 1974

119. *He Went Against the Peace Pipe,* Larry McMurty. The New York Review of Books, Vol. 55, No. 3, March 6, 2008

120. *George Armstrong Custer,* Frederick Dellenbaugh. Macmillan Co., New York, 1926

121. *Custer: Man and Legend,* William Heuman Dodd. Mead &Co., New York, 1968

122. *Tom Custer - Ride to Glory,* Carl Day. Arthur Clark Co., Spokane, WA, 2002

123. *Son of the Morning Star,* Evan Connell. Perennial Library, NY, 1985

124. *Eyewitnesses to the Indian Wars 1865-1890,* Volume 4, Peter Cozzens. Stack Pole Books, 2001

125. *Centennial Campaign,* John Gray. The Old Army Press, Fort Collins, CO, 1976

126. *When Custer Walked the Streets of Old Monroe,* Richard Micka and Steve Alexander. Monroe, MI, 2004

127. *The Gallant Custer: A Talk with his Father-Some Interesting Reminiscences-His Younger Brother,* Daily Evening Bulletin. San Francisco, CA, Monday July 31, 1876

128. *Custer's Last Fight,* David Evans. Upton and Sons, El Segundo, CA, 1999

129. *Soldiers Falling Into Camp,* Robert Kammen, Joe Marshall, Frederick Lefthand. Affiliated Writers of America Encampment, WY, 1992

130. *Bismarck, D. T.,* Kim Fundingsland. Niess Impressions, Minot, ND, 2009

131. *In Custer's Shadow: Major Marcus Reno,* Ronald Nichols. Old Army Press, Fort Collins, CO, 1999

132. *The Custer Trail,* Frank Anders. Arthur Clark Co., Glendale, CA, 1983

133. *General Custer and the Battle of the Little Big Horn: The Federal View,* John Carroll. Carroll & Co., Bryan, TX, 1986

134. *Custer's Last Battle,* Richard Roberts. Monroe County Library System, 1978

135. *Old Neutriment,* Glendolin Wagner. University of Nebraska Press, Lincoln, NE, 1989

136. *Vanishing Victory,* Bruce Liddic. Upton & Sons Publishers, El Segundo, CA, 2004

137. *Rations, Forage, & Ammunition: Logistical Problems Facing the Dakota Column in the Summer of 1876,* Jim Schneider. Research Review: The Journal of the Little Big Horn Associates, Vol. 5, No. 2, June 1991

138. *A Picture Report of the Custer Fight,* William Reusswig. Hasting House Publishers, NY, 1967

139. *Custer Should Have Gone Fishing,* M. R. Montgomery. Sports Afield, July, 1995

140. *Custer's Last Battle,* Edward Godfrey. Outbooks, Olympic Valley, CA, 1976

141. *Little Big Horn Diary,* James Willert Upton & Sons Publishers, El Segundo, CA, 1997

142. *The Custer Mystery,* W. Donald Horn Research Review The Journal of the Little Big Horn Associates Vol. 18 No. 2 Summer, 2004

143. *The ABCs of Custer's Last Stand,* Arthur Unger. Upton & Sons Publishers, El Segundo, CA ,2004

144. *The Custer Companion,* Thom Hatch. Stackpole Books, Mechanicsburg, PA, 2002

145. *General Terry's Last Statement to Custer,* John Manion. Monroe County Library System, Monroe, MI, 1983

146. *Massacre: The Custer Cover-Up,* W. Kent King. Upton & Sons Publishers, El Segundo, CA, 1989

147. *With Custer on the Little Bighorn,* William Taylor. Viking Penguin, NY, 1996

148. *Little Big Horn Diary,* James Willert. Upton & Sons Publishers, El Segundo, CA, 1997

149. *The Custer Myth,* Colonel W. A. Graham. Bonanza Books, NY, 1953

150. *Echoes of the Little Bighorn,* David Humphreys Miller. American Heritage, Vol. 12, No. 4, June 1971

151. *Reno and Apsaalooka Survive Custer,* Ottie Reno. Cornwall Books, NY, 1997

152. *It is a Good Day to Die,* Herman Viola. University of Nebraska Press, Lincoln, NE, 1998

153. *Deep Ravine Trail,* Neil Mangum. Custer Battlefield National Monument, Crow Agency, MT, 1982

154. *Little Big Horn Rendezvous,* Clarence Belue. Published by the author, Madison, WI, 1992

155. *The Custer Battle Casualties, II,* Richard Hardorff. Upton & Sons Publishers, El Segundo, CA, 1999

156. *A Sad and Terrible Blunder,* Roger Darling. Potomac-Western Press, Vienna, VA 1990

157. *The Conquest of the Missouri,* Joseph Hanson. A. C. McClurg & Co., Chicago, 1909

158. *The Little Big Horn Survivors,* Charles Cook. Research Review: The Journal of the Little Big Horn Associates, Vol. 5, No. 1, January 1991

159. *Custer: Cavalier in Buckskin,* Robert Utley. University of Oklahoma Press, Norman, OK, 2001

160. *First Scalp for Custer,* Paul Hedron. University of Nebraska Press, Lincoln, NE, 1980

161. *Speaking of Custer...!,* Tippecanoe Jack Hurless. Harrison News Herald, Cadiz, OH, May 30, 2005

162. *Libbie Keeps Her Promise: Addressing the Custer Story,* Dr. Lawrence Frost. Garry Owen Publishers, Monroe, MI, 1980

163. *What Valor Is; Legacy: New Perspectives on the Battle of the Little Bighorn,* Brian Dippie. Montana Historical Society Press, Helena, MT, 1996

164. *Custer's List,* Don Russell. Amon Carter Museum of Western Art, Fort Worth, TX, 1969

165. *The Custer Reader,* Paul Hutton. University of Nebraska Press, Lincoln, NE, 1992

166. *Sioux Chief Sitting Bull Killed: Led Victory over Custer at Little Big Horn,* John Kirshon. American History website

167. *The Great Chiefs,* Benjamin Capps. Time-Life Books, New York, 1975

168. *Aunt Elizabeth As I Knew Her.* Colonel Brice C. W. Custer Newsletter Little Big Horn Associates April 1968 Vol. 2 No. 4 as Compiled by Ronald C. Pickard in Reprint of the Newsletter Volume Two. January-June 1968.

169. *A History of the Indians of the United States.* Angie Debo University of Oklahoma Press, Norman OK 1970.

Amidst the smoke and din of battle the Author makes a valiant stand at Medicine Tail Coulee in this 2004. Courtesy of Steve Shaw.

The end of Yellow Hair during Arts and Entertainment's "George Armstrong Custer: America's Golden Cavalier". Courtesy of Mary Desson.

THE FILMOGRAPHY AND TELEVISION SPECIALS OF STEVE ALEXANDER

1. *Slices of Life: Battle of Bristo Station,*
Michigan Public Television, 1990

2. *Custer's Last Stand,*
Hardin Chamber of Commerce and Agriculture, 1990

3. *Montana Trilogy,*
KXLY presentation, 1990

4. *Fort Custer, Getting to Know You,*
Lawrence Productions, 1991

5. *Cascades '92 Civil War Muster,*
Public Broadcast Special, 1992

6. *Hardin: In the Heart of the American West,* Hardin,
Montana Chamber of Commerce and Agriculture, 1992

7. *Along the Little Big Horn,*
Special presentation KTVX 4, Utah, 1993

8. *Jack Palance: Legends of the West,*
Vidmark Entertainment, 1993

9. *Custer-The Story of Yellow Hair,*
Cromwell Productions, 1994

10. *Custer's Monroe-The Nickel Tour,*
Major Vista Media, 1995

11. *American Visions: The Wilderness and the West,*
BBC-2, 1995

12. *Red Gold, Black Hills,*
Great Western Films, 1995

13. *Amazing America,*
The Learning Channel-Four Point Entertainment, 1995

14. *Fort Abraham Lincoln,*
North Dakota Tourism, 1997

15. *Montana Beneath the Big Sky,*
Third Eye Productions, 1997

16. *Biography: George Armstrong Custer-America's Golden
Cavalier,* A&E-Greystone Productions, 1997

17. *The New Explorers: Betrayal at Little Big Horn,*
A&E-Kurtis Productions, 1998.

18. *The Western Edge,* Dakota Communications/Fort
Abraham Lincoln Foundation, 1998

19. *Little Big Horn - The Untold Story,*
History Channel-Lou Reda Productions, 1999

20. *Encounters with the Unexplained: Custer's Last Stand,
What Really Happened at the Little Big Horn?*
Pax Channel-Grizzly Adams Productions, 2000

21. *First In Battle: The True Story of the 7ᵗʰ Cavalry,*
History Channel, 2001

22. *C-Span: The Writings of Black Elk,*
National Cable Satellite Corporation, 2001

23. *Custer Coal Mine: Fond Memories,* Community Access
Television, Cable 12, Bismarck, North Dakota 2001

24. *Playset Video Collector: The Westerns,*
Atomic Home Video, 2002

25. *Carson & Cody: The Hunter Heroes,*
History Channel-Native Sun Productions, 2003

26. *Command Decisions #115 Battle of Little Bighorn,*
History Channel-Michael Hoff Productions, 2004

27. *Only in America: Custer's Last Stand Battle Reenactors,*
Discovery Times, 2004

28. *Wild West Tech: Military Tech,*
History Channel-Greystone Productions, 2004

29. *Pow Wow Trail: Episode 10 -
The White Man's Indian,* I. C. E. Productions, 2004

30. *Custer VS Hampton Huntertown,*
Pennsylvania Cable Network, 2005

31. *History Hogs: On the Trail of General Custer,*
History Channel-GRB Entertainment, 2005

32. *The Presidents,*
History Channel-Greystone Productions, 2005

33. *Monterey Pass,* Pennsylvania Cable Network, 2006

34. *Investigating History: Who Killed Crazy Horse?,*
History Channel-Kurtis Productions, 2005

35. *Gettysburg: Darkest Days & Finest Hours,* Lion Heart
Productions, 2008

36. *The Battle of Hanover,* Hanover Multimedia, 2008

37. *The Great Indian Wars 1540-1890,* Mill Creek
Entertainment, 2009

38. *What Went Down at Custer's Last Stand,*
History Channel, 2009

39. *Bighorn,* Monorail Pictures and Left Bank Films 2010

40. *Mystery Files,*
Parthenon, 2011